HOW TO STOP NEGATIVE THINKING

THE 7-STEP PLAN TO ELIMINATE NEGATIVITY, OVERCOME RUMINATION, CEASE OVERTHINKING SPIRAL, AND CHANGE YOUR TOXIC THOUGHTS TO HEALTHY SELF-TALK

CHASE HILL

CONTENTS

A FREE GIFT TO OUR READERS

29 WAYS TO OVERCOME NEGATIVE THOUGHTS

I'd like to give you a gift as a way of saying thanks for your purchase!

In 29 Ways to Overcome Negative Thoughts, you'll discover:

- 10 Strategies to Reduce Negativity in Your Life
- 7 Steps to Quickly Stop Negative Thoughts

- 12 Powerful Tips to Beat Negative Thinking

To receive your Free Ebook, visit the link:

free.chasehillbooks.com

Prefer a quick access? Scan the QR code below:

If you have any difficulty downloading the ebook, contact me at **chase@chasehillbooks.com,** and I'll send you a copy as soon as possible.

INTRODUCTION

Lisa had reached the end of her rope. She was fed up with people telling her to stop being so negative, as if it were her choice.

Tom knew that his negativity weighed him down, but too many clichés like "life is what you make it" caused him to completely cut himself off from the world.

The pandemic had filled Jason with so much fear and negativity that he became agoraphobic and couldn't bring himself to leave the house.

Sammi had reached a point where she wasn't sure that life was worth fighting for as every moment of her life was so bleak.

And there are thousands, if not millions, of people who have their own personal struggles with negativity.

The problem with negativity is that it isn't simply a bad mood that you can shake off when you feel like it.

Rumination starts, the mind begins to dwell, fear and anxiety take over.

We look for inspiration in the world, anything to shine a bit of light, but that doesn't happen. Over time, you start to notice that there is more negative thinking going on than positive, like a sponge soaking up all the bad. Sadly, negative thinking becomes a permanent state of mind that can wreak havoc on all areas of your life.

If you feel like you are walking on the very edge of a cliff and that one more issue is likely to cause you to fall, you aren't alone.

According to the National Science Foundation, 80% of our thoughts are negative. If we have an average of 12,000 to 50,000 thoughts per day, that's between 9,600 to 40,000 negative thoughts a day. That is exhausting, to say the least. We are literally swimming in our negative thoughts and many of us are drowning.

Negativity isn't like a broken leg or a skin rash. You can't see it, but you carry it around with you all the time. Not everyone can afford therapy or is comfortable with the idea of talking to a stranger. Others are worried that they will be labeled and just given anti-depressants.

There are also plenty of people who feel that they deserve to live with such suffering or even feel guilty for feeling the way they do. Nothing could be further from the truth! Everyone deserves to have a happy life that they feel in control of. My goal is to let you see this in a simple, effective, yet proven way.

My first book *How to Stop Overthinking* became a bestseller and sparked great interest in other issues that wonderful readers were willing to share with us. More specifically, so many of you responded to the chapter on negative thinking.

Since then, the pandemic, natural disasters, and financial insecurity have caused a sharp rise in negative thinking. So, it's time to take a more in-depth look at how we tackle negative thinking and constant worrying.

I felt that people who were engulfed in negativity needed a straightforward plan that could be broken down and followed in smaller steps. And so, the L.I.B.E.R.T.Y. system came to my mind. Just 7 simple steps to help you understand where your thoughts come from and how to start seeing the changes you want to see.

Throughout this book, we are going to gain a deeper understanding that will allow you to:

L—Learn how your brain works

I—Inspect your thought patterns

B—Beat negative thinking

E—Eliminate rumination and overthinking

R—Rewire your brain, rule your mind, and reduce stress

T—Throw away negativity and worrying

Y—Yield positive changes

In 7 chapters, you will be able to understand why your brain functions the way it does and where these negative thoughts stem from. We will look at the patterns and habits we fall into. There will be easy-to-follow techniques and practice exercises every step of the way so that you feel fully supported and prepared from the comfort of your own home.

Toward the end of the book, we won't just talk about positive thinking but how you can make changes so that you are taking care of yourself in every aspect of your life so that you feel energized and ready to build new and exciting relationships and take on all the opportunities available to you.

I have been where you are. I hit rock bottom and I stayed there for far too long. Because I would dwell on every decision, I got stuck in a rut that made me doubt everything about my life from which cereal to have for breakfast to the direction I was heading.

My girlfriend found my lack of confidence infuriating and left. I missed out on a promotion because I thought that I wasn't good enough and I started to resent my work. Everything was making me so angry, but I couldn't find the strength to clear my mind.

When it dawned on me that I had nobody I could really call a friend, I knew that something had to be done. After researching, studying, and learning what not to do, I started to make small changes that led to bigger improvements.

I promised myself that not only would I never go back to that dark place, but that I would also promise to help others to do the same thing. My love for psychology encouraged me to make a massive career change and become a certified life coach and social interaction specialist. The more people I helped, the more motivated I was to delve into other areas, which led me to where I am today.

I have read numerous books on negativity, thought patterns, and making changes in your life. I found all of them to have their own benefits and my head was nodding in agreement with the authors. But the changes never came.

I realized that understanding something was not the same as putting it into practice. Because of this, you will find the science behind the way we think as well as activities that you can try along the way to feel the difference. Understanding what negativity bias is doesn't mean you have the tools to break the cycle. In this book, you will find the tools.

Making this type of change in your life is never easy. It requires determination, commitment, and patience. You need to learn how to forgive yourself and begin by putting one foot in front of the other. It's not a case of waking up tomorrow and things will be different. If it were that simple, nobody would suffer from negative thinking.

At the same time, as long as you are prepared to do the work in this book, you are 7 steps away from a better life. Our first step is to understand why our brain gets stuck in a continuous cycle of negative thinking.

CHAPTER 1: LEARN WHY YOUR BRAIN IS HARDWIRED FOR NEGATIVITY

The first thing we have to gain control over is berating ourselves for our negative thought patterns. All those people that have told you that you are just a negative person, and you aren't trying to be positive, are wrong. Science tells us that our brain is trained to pay more attention to our negative thoughts. To an extent, there is a good reason for this.

On the one hand, when we are stressed or feeling scared, our brain releases the hormones cortisol and adrenaline. These two hormones play a crucial role in the fight or flight response. The fight or flight response is what protects us from danger. If your child crosses the road, the first response is to grab their hand and probably shout at them because we fear an accident—even if no car is coming. On the other hand, too much cortisol can have numerous consequences on our health. Some of these include:

• Weight gain

- Acne

- Thinning skin

- Easy bruising

- Muscle weakness

- Severe fatigue

- High blood pressure

- Headaches

Increased blood pressure, headaches, weight gain, and severe anxiety are also symptoms of too much adrenaline. You are also more at risk of heart attacks and strokes. So, the release of cortisol and adrenaline is generally a good thing, but as soon as negative thinking becomes a serious issue, we are putting our health at risk.

There is another problem with an overactive fight or flight response. An increase in cortisol increases white matter in the brain. White matter is good for communication between the gray matter of the brain, but it's the gray matter that carries out processes. Gray matter is necessary to cope with stress effectively. When white matter dominates, along with increased stress and fear, it becomes harder for us to decipher complex problems.

Those who don't suffer from negative thinking might be able to take a step back and view situations from alternative perspectives. In our heightened states, this is much more difficult.

We also have to consider that although our brain is an organ, it acts like a muscle in the sense that it needs training. Through no fault of our own, our brain has been trained in the wrong way. Our negative thoughts are processed in the right prefrontal cortex, just above your right eye. On the top, left-hand side of the brain, we have the left prefrontal cortex.

Thanks to technology that scans the brain, we can see that people who suffer from depression have an overdeveloped right prefrontal cortex and an underdeveloped left prefrontal cortex. Imagine lifting weights with only your right arm—your left will never be able to keep up.

But as the brain is not a muscle, how does this actually work? The brain contains approximately 100 billion neurons, and each neuron has an average of 7,000 synapses (connections to other neurons). All our negative thoughts and experiences get stored as memories. Every time we recall a memory, the synapses are strengthened. The more often these memories are accessed, the quicker and easier it is for negative thoughts to reappear (Crawford, n.d.).

Can the Brain Really Be Biased?

Negativity bias goes back to our ancestors and their need to be cautious of danger in the environment. Their survival depended on it. Of course, we have come a long way since we were cavemen hunting or being hunted. There is no need for us to be constantly on the lookout for danger, but this is an automatic process that starts to develop as infants and for some of us, the process is heightened to such an extent that negativity consumes us.

This negativity bias has been studied by psychologists for years. John Cacioppo, Ph.D., from the University of Chicago, studied electrical activity in the brain's cerebral cortex. Participants in his study were shown images that stimulated positive emotions and others that stimulated negative emotions. The negative stimuli caused a greater surge in electrical activity than the positive stimuli.

Neuropsychologist Rick Hanson, Ph.D., confirmed that the amygdala (the area of the brain that controls our emotions and motivation) uses approximately two-thirds of its neurons to detect negativity.

This means that two-thirds of your emotions and motivation are focused on the negative—the very definition of bias!

What's more, the amygdala then takes these super-charged, dominant-negative neurons and very quickly stores them in the long-term memory. This is why we tend to remember negative or traumatic experiences more than positive ones. Why it's easier to remember an insult than a compliment. And why we think negatively more often than we do positively.

Cacioppo's research also found that we are more likely to make decisions based on negative information than we are positive information. Furthermore, negativity has a greater impact on our motivation. If you set goals, there is a greater chance that you will focus on what you will have to give up to achieve the goal instead of what you will gain from reaching it. (Cacioppo et al., 2014).

Imagine you have an argument with your friend or your partner. Even if the argument has been resolved, do you focus on the negative memories, experiences, and qualities or do you think back to all the good times you have had and why you love them? The brain is wired to think about the negative.

Why Do People Ruminate?

There is a difference between overthinking and ruminating. When we overthink, we are spending more time than necessary thinking about an emotion, action, or experience. A woman choosing her wedding dress is probably going to overthink because it is such an important decision. The decision isn't surrounded by negativity. Rumination is the act of overthinking about negative feelings, things that have occurred, or things that may or may not occur. Examples of rumination include the continuous thinking about:

• A night out when you drank too much and did something stupid

• A mistake you made during a presentation

• Failing an exam

• Having an argument with a loved one

• The fear of getting ill

• The fear of losing your job/a friend/a partner

• Global warming and the world coming to an end

• An upcoming social event where you will have to talk to strangers

- What if... and if only...

The list is endless because it very much depends on the individual. Some people may laugh at those who ruminate on the state of the planet, perhaps call them dramatic. But others might consider someone to be dramatic for worrying about things that are now in the past.

While talking to clients from all backgrounds with varying degrees of negative thinking, I put together a list of the most common, harmful negative thoughts that we ruminate over:

- I will never be able to do that

- They are better than me

- I failed/I'm a failure

- I will never forgive them

- I should have done something differently

- It's too late

- This is going to be a disaster

- It's far too difficult

- It ruined my whole day

One of the most common causes of rumination is that we feel like we are doing something about a problem. If you fear losing your job and live every day on eggshells expecting it to be your last day in the office, rumination takes over your mind. Our subconscious feels that by thinking about this problem, replaying different scenarios, we are seeking answers to prevent job loss. The initial fear of losing your job is replaced by what our mind believes is proactive problem-solving.

"If a problem is fixable, if a situation is such that you can do something about it, then there is no need to worry. If it's not fixable, then there is no help in worrying. There is no benefit in worrying whatsoever."

— DALAI LAMA

It's easy coming from someone who has such an enlightened state of mind. For the average human, rumination and worrying is not something that we can simply switch off. While everyone is going to worry about things at some point in their lives, when the worrying becomes problematic, i.e., it affects their work and relationships, it can develop into generalized anxiety disorder (GAD). GAD affects 6.8 million adults in the U.S. What is more concerning is that 25.1% of children between 13 and 18 are also affected by anxiety disorders (ADAA, n.d.).

Put It into Practice

A quick exercise for you. Think back to last week or last month and list 10 things you had worried would occur this week or this month. Now think about how many of them actually occurred. I will take a typical list of what I would worry about.

I was going to oversleep **X**

I was going to make a mistake with a new client **X**

I wouldn't be able to make it through my gym class **X**

The metro would crash **X**

My parents were going to nag me about spending time with them ✓

My parents were going to get sick **X**

I wouldn't have enough money to save toward my holiday **X**

My friends were going to laugh at my haircut **X**

My boss was going to fire me **X**

I was going to burn the dinner for friends that weekend **X**

One of my 10 worries came true and even this one was pretty much out of my control. This is in line with data on the validity of our worries.

According to researchers at the Pennsylvania State University, 91.4% of worries didn't come true for GAD sufferers (LaFreniere & Newman, 2018). Which links back to negativity bias. Our brains are trained to think the worst and despite our logical intelligence, this natural occurrence is hard to stop.

Typical Mistakes People Make When Dealing with Negative Thoughts

Again, when we look at mistakes we have made with our negative thoughts, it's not another reason to feel bad about ourselves. What has happened has happened and we can't change that. Being aware of common mistakes helps us to avoid making them in the future. If you read this while nodding your head, you can know that you aren't alone.

1) You see things in black and white

It's not always one or the other, right or wrong, happy or sad, good or bad. Life is far too messy to see things in just black and white. Rather than labeling something as either positive or negative, we need to see things as just what they are. When focused on one extreme or the other, we miss out on a wide range in between; this gray area can help us to see things in a different light and make better decisions.

It's also easier to make small changes when you stop seeing only black and white. Today you are feeling negative. There are a lot of steps in between negative and positive. To aim to be positive tomorrow might be a huge step that is just too big. Instead, tomorrow, we need to aim to be OK; the next day, good; the following happy; and so on.

2) You brush your negativity under the rug

Out of sight out of mind! But this isn't the case with our negative thoughts. You might be able to push them to one side, but this won't resolve the problem. Ignoring the problem or pretending it doesn't exist can make it worse.

3) You tell yourself that things are out of your control

In many cases, this might be true. We have certainly seen how quickly control can be taken away from us over the last 18 months. The pandemic has taken people from us, cost us our jobs, even our homes, and for a long time, our freedom. Feeling like you are out of control is scary, but you have to remember there is always one thing that you can control: how you react.

4) You assume and make incorrect predictions

When thinking about what could happen, we tap into our memories to look for past experiences.

If someone eats shellfish and gets food poisoning, they will recall this memory before eating shellfish again. If you go horseback riding and fall off, before going riding again, you are going to wonder if the same thing is going to happen.

There is no evidence to suggest history will repeat itself. But because our negative memories are so predominant, topped with the tendency to think negatively, we will fall into the habit of predicting incorrect outcomes.

5) You see negativity only as negative

This is a good one, but have you ever thought about how negativity and anxiety work in your favor? You assume that you are going to miss your flight, so you create a backup plan. Walking home alone makes you anxious, so you take a cab, which is safer.

I'm not saying that we should celebrate the negative thoughts we have because there has to be a limit. It is important to realize that we also don't want a life that is 100% positive and that, like our ancestors, our anxiety and negativity can keep us a little bit cautious.

6) Your focus is on overcoming negativity rather than improving self-care

Negative thinking is interlinked with multiple other issues. Our confidence is rock-bottom; we don't like who we see in the mirror or don't even recognize who we are. You're constantly stressed and tired. While we want to reduce the amount of time we spend ruminating, we also need to start looking after ourselves in a way we deserve.

Finding the Positive Needle in the Negative Haystack

Generally speaking, negativity is breeding and spreading like never before. This is thanks to the news, internet, and social media. When the Black Death began in Europe in October 1347, news of its deadliness wouldn't have reached the Americas. And it wouldn't have been on the news 24 hours a day.

In fact, thanks to the Olympics, we have recently had some inspiring international stories. But even then, there are people determined to spread negativity. We miss the days when social media was used to be sociable rather than feed the fears and hatred of others.

It's not all doom and gloom. If you look hard enough, you can see people in the world trying to make a difference. Companies replanting trees, countries welcoming those displaced by war, and the amusing images that do nothing except make us smile. Social media isn't all bad. Movements like #BlackLivesMatter and #MeToo enable global involvement to put an end to unjust behavior. It might be a negative haystack, but the positive needle is still there. The same is true for our negative thinking.

Just as scientists have spent a long time researching how the brain is wired and why we are prone to negativity, researchers are also looking at proven ways that we can overcome negative thinking patterns and even break the negative bias cycle. Some of the methods you might have tried before, and naturally, you are thinking that if they didn't work before, they aren't going to work this time.

Not every method works for everyone, which is why we are going to go over 7 simple steps, but each step will have various strategies to match different personalities. Even if you have tried strategies before, try again with an open mind. It might be that the first time you weren't mentally prepared, or you hadn't fully understood the root cause of your negative thinking.

Now that we have a solid understanding of negativity and rumination, and that our brains are wired in this particular way, we can begin to look at different thought patterns and clearly define where our negative thinking is stemming from. You might want to have a pen and paper handy for the next chapter!

CHAPTER 2: INSPECT YOUR THOUGHT PATTERNS WITH 3 EASY-TO-USE TOOLS

J ust because we now understand how the brain is wired, it doesn't mean we can stop negative thoughts from taking over.

While the first chapter was more of an understanding of why we shouldn't punish ourselves for the way we are, this chapter takes a more in-depth look into recognizing our thought patterns, so it becomes easier to prevent rumination with the strategies in the following chapter.

The Characteristics of Negative Thinking and Identifying Problems

It helps to understand the two main mindsets that people tend to have. A healthy mindset is a growth mindset. This is when we believe that our own abilities and intelligence can be developed over time. A fixed mindset is one where you believe you will never master a new skill or that you just aren't good enough to achieve something.

Unfortunately, with negative thinking, we are often stuck in a fixed mindset where we feel that this is never going to change. One of the first exercises we will look at in the next chapter is how to develop a growth mindset so that you actually believe you can change your way of thinking.

We can break down our negative thinking into 5 core categories:

• Automatic thoughts are those that just suddenly appear, and it may even feel like they came out of nowhere.

• Distorted negative thoughts are based on no evidence or facts and they are often wrong.

• Believable negativity comes from facts. or at least things that you perceive as being true.

• If you notice unhelpful negative thoughts, you may find that they influence your behavior. As we saw that decision-making is impacted by our negativity, this category can be dangerous because we do things that may not lead us toward our goals.

• Finally, intrusive negative thoughts are normally frightening, violent, or the worst-case scenario of everything. This type of thinking can lead to anxiety and panic attacks as they are extremely difficult to stop.

Furthermore, there are 12 negative thought patterns that we can identify:

1. All or nothing: As mentioned before, this is our black-and-white thinking. Your friends either love you or hate you, you are going to excel at your presentation or completely flunk it.

2. Over-generalization: This is very much a fixed-mindset pattern. You may have had one negative experience and see this as a sign that everything will turn out the same. You had one bad date so there is no point in going on anymore because they will all be bad.

3. The mental filter: Like a colander, your mind lets all the positive elements slip through and only grasps the negative. We experience this with constructive criticism; although there are good comments, it's the negative ones that stick.

4. Rejecting the positive: You may have told yourself positive things but discounted them as irrelevant. You lost 2 pounds, but it doesn't count because you skipped dinner the previous night.

5. Making assumptions: This can seem very much like paranoia or irrational fears, despite feeling very real to you. A common example is our health. If a food doesn't taste the same, we might assume it's COVID-19 despite having no other symptoms. These patterns fall into the distorted thought category.

6. Clairvoyance: We wrongfully read the minds of others, but their thoughts are always going to be negative toward us. People think we are stupid, overweight, strange, etc.

7. Fortune telling: You don't need a crystal ball because you know what the future holds. But these predictions aren't based on fact, they are based on negative thinking. Nobody is going to like you at yoga class, so there is no point in going. You aren't going to get the promotion, so it's silly to put your name forward.

8. Exaggerating: The negativities are magnified. You might have made a mistake and you make it out to be more than it really is, but it can also be found when looking at the successes of others. We have to be careful with social media here because it's easy to exaggerate the achievements or happiness of others because of a photo.

9. Minimalizing: Similar to discounting positives, we can look at our successes and not celebrate them for what they really are. For example, you might pay off all of your debts but rather than see this as a great thing, you focus on the fact that you don't have any savings, or you are angry because you got yourself into debt in the first place.

10. The perfectionist: Expecting to get everything just right all the time is humanly impossible. We are flawed creatures and we will make mistakes. Setting unrealistic goals can lead to anger and frustration, and adds to the fixed mindset that you can't do something.

11. Self-blame: In reality, you can only be hard on yourself for the things that you are responsible for. When things go wrong that aren't your fault or are out of your control, the only thing you can do is be responsible for your emotions; you can't blame yourself for these situations.

12. Negative labels: Whether it's because of mistakes or trying to be perfect, you label yourself as weak, bad, and irresponsible, and you tell yourself that you deserve the things you are going through.

I can't emphasize enough that if you are stuck in a place where this type of thinking occurs, it isn't your fault. We have already seen that our brain prefers to look at the negative side of things. However, there is another reason why it is more difficult for us to change our perspective so that we are able to see the complete picture.

Mental models play a significant role in how we view the world and the decisions we make are based on this. If our mental models are limited, we may end up stuck in this tunnel vision of negativity.

Mental Models

When it comes to understanding the world, there are a great number of complexities. To help us comprehend aspects of life, the connections between events and emotions, and the opportunities we have, there are mental models.

Mental models help us to arrange sections of information so that reality is clearer. Many of us notice that the lack of clarity is what makes even the simplest of choices challenging. With a clearer, more realistic understanding of what is going on in our lives, we are better able to make the right decisions.

Mental models are like pieces of Lego. There is not a great deal you can do with only a couple of pieces. You have a greater advantage when you have more pieces.

Take a school environment. The government sets targets without stepping into the classroom, then the teacher tries to implement learning in a fun way while complying with government standards. The students are lost in standardized testing and ineffective learning strategies and the parents are frustrated about grades and homework.

Each person has their mental model for seeing the situation, but the person who is able to see all mental models is the one who can come up with the best solutions.

There are hundreds of mental models from numeracy to human nature. It helps us to learn about some of the mental models of core thinking concepts. To improve your decision-making skills, you want to try and adopt as many of these mental models as possible.

1. The map of your reality

No map is ever perfectly accurate. When you look at your reality, it's important to appreciate that the map you have created isn't going to be perfect. Maps are reductions of territories and are subject to change. These could be significant changes that alter reality completely or small changes that throw a monkey wrench in the works. Either way, the map is not fixed and may well be out of date.

2. Reasoning from first principles

When it comes to problem-solving, it's easy to get lost in all the factors of that problem. Within each problem, you will find facts, ideas, and assumptions. If you can peel each layer back and separate these factors, you are left with only the information that is true and relevant. By going back to the first principle of any problem, you can discover solutions based on accurate information.

3. Thought experiments

We can use our imagination to explore and experiment with all that can be known. One of the most famous thought experiments was Galileo's balls. He didn't actually drop balls from the Leaning Tower of Pisa to understand gravity and acceleration. He created a thought process that allowed him to explore hypotheses. Using thought experiments allows you to hypothesize situations, learn from mistakes, and evaluate consequences to avoid other mistakes in the future.

4. First- vs. second-order thinking

If I drop a cup it will smash. This is the immediate consequence or first-order. But what happens later on down the road? What are the subsequent results of my actions? That cup was a gift from my gran, a memory that I can't get back. All my other cups aren't big enough to give me the caffeine boost I need. This is a very simplified example. However, if you train yourself to think beyond the immediate result, you can plan more effectively.

5. Probability

Probability uses science and numbers to understand the likely outcome of something. It's an incredible mental model for negative thinkers because it provides undeniable logic. Imagine you read a headline that says burglaries have doubled in Washington, D.C. The immediate thought is that Washington isn't safe and you don't want to go there.

When you look at the probability of being burgled, it's 0.11% (FBI UCR, 2019). If the headline were true, the probability of you being burgled is still only 0.22%. Our decisions are far more accurate when we find numbers to back our beliefs.

6. Inversion

Inversion is a technique whereby we invert our problems and think backward rather than forward. Typically, we would face a problem from the starting point, but if you begin at the end, you can see what obstacles may arise and remove them before they occur.

7. Occam's razor

Occam's razor simply states that if you have two theories and the outcomes are the same, it is always best to choose the simplest theory. This is not to say the simplest answer is the correct one. In some cases, there is a need for critical thinking, more so in scientific applications. If we go back to our health and you have a headache, the simplest explanation is dehydration rather than a brain tumor.

8. Hanlon's razor

In our negative minds, it's easy to assume the worst and this often encourages paranoia. Hanlon's razor states that we shouldn't assume an act is evil or unkind when it could be stupidity. If a colleague forgets to give you credit for your efforts, it may not be that they are trying to step over you, it's more likely that they weren't smart enough or empathetic enough to consider how you would feel.

Again, like Occam's razor, it's not always the case as there are plenty of toxic people out to work the system to their advantage, but we can use this model to lessen the pain of some of our negative thoughts and give people the benefit of the doubt.

9. Your circle of competence

Maybe there is something you can see yourself as an expert in, there will be a large number of things that you are good at (even though it is hard to list them now) and there are other things that you have little to no knowledge of. If your mindset is fixed, you won't be able to see that there are areas that are lacking, but you can learn and improve. Sometimes, we need to learn more before we can make a sound decision.

These are 9 of the most effective mental models that can be beneficial in combating negative thinking patterns. Don't try to master them all at once because too many radical changes will be hard to maintain. The trick is always to take one strategy or technique, practice and master it, and then add others.

3 Intuitive Tools to Test Yourself

To test yourself on negative thought patterns, you have to first remember that this is an automatic process that you have no control over. When something pops into your mind, it is what it is. You can rehash the thought and try to see it in a more positive light, you can underestimate its importance or overestimate it; this often comes with rumination after the initial thought.

To clearly define whether you have a problem with negative thinking, you have to be incredibly honest about your negative thoughts.

For example, if you open your bank account and there is only $100, what is that first gut reaction?

There are degrees of negativity, a spectrum on its own. The more honest you can answer the questions, the more clarity you will get when understanding the extent of your negativity.

Intuitive tool #1

A nice simple tool to start with is the list of 12 negative pattern characteristics we saw previously in this chapter. Take a pen and paper and copy the following bullet points:

- All or nothing
- Over-generalization
- The mental filter
- Rejecting the positive
- Making assumptions
- Clairvoyance
- Fortune telling
- Exaggerating
- Minimalizing
- The perfectionist
- Self-blame

- Negative labels

See if you can associate your negative thinking with each of the above; give real examples based on an accurate recall of situations. If you keep a journal, it's a good idea to go back and look at things you have written about rather than relying on memory alone. Don't force it though; if you can't think of an example, just leave it blank.

If you can identify with three or more of the negative pattern characteristics, you need to take proactive steps to make changes. The more you can identify with, the deeper your problem goes.

If you only identify with one or two, that's not to say you don't have negative tendencies, and you can still implement our techniques to experience a more joyful life.

Intuitive tool #2

Because of automatic thinking, our negativity is sometimes hidden. We cover it, bury it, only let it out at suitable times or just pretend that it isn't there. The following 20 statements can be ranked as never, sometimes, and always.

1. Change makes me nervous and I prefer things to stay as they are.

2. I will take over when other people are trying to do things because I can do it better.

3. I need a plan before I do anything.

4. When I make a plan, I need to follow each step.

5. I firmly believe that everything will turn out according to my plan.

6. There needs to be a logical reason for me to do something.

7. I use a lot of negative contractions like can't, don't, and wouldn't.

8. I often doubt my own abilities.

9. I spend a long time trying to come to a decision.

10. I say things but don't follow through with them.

11. I experience a lot of negative emotions like anger, jealousy, and sadness.

12. The future is uncertain and concerning.

13. When I consider the present, I am often influenced by my past mistakes.

14. I feel the need to be right all the time.

15. Because of my need to be right, I only trust myself.

16. I find it difficult to believe what others say.

17. I can't completely trust anyone or even myself.

18. I'm not happy if I don't reach my goals.

19. I make judgments of others based on my standards.

20. I am stubborn when it comes to getting what I want.

There is a deeper meaning to each question that goes beyond positive and negative. But before looking at these meanings, double-check that you have answered every question honestly.

1. A fear of change is going to keep you in a fixed mindset. You can't stop changes from occurring and it's better to adopt a flexible attitude rather than fighting the inevitable.

2. Trying to control everything is exhausting both physically and mentally. We need to learn how to hand control over to others, accept that some things can't be controlled, and focus on what we can control to achieve our goals.

3. Having a plan is a good thing, but there is a problem when you have to plan and rationalize everything you do. It stops us from enjoying the moment and can often set us up for failure when our plans depend on others.

4. Again, to an extent, this is a good thing but only when not taken to the extreme. If you become obsessed with the steps of your plans, your goals might be too rigid with no room for adapting the plan. It goes back to not everything being in your control.

5. If our plan is flawed (which is very possible if our thinking is predominantly negative), we are going to be extremely disappointed if things don't go our way. Our focus is still too much on the outcomes instead of enjoying the process and living in the moment.

6. A little bit of logic is sensible, but if we go to the extreme of not doing something because it's not 100% logical, we start to ignore our own intuition and can miss out on amazing experiences.

7. Negative words keep you in a negative frame of mind. They program your brain into a way of thinking, and it becomes a struggle to see anything other than what the words are telling you.

8. The same as negative words. They cloud our reality and make it hard to see things in any other way.

9. Being indecisive delays change and is often a smokescreen to put off something you are scared of doing or trying. Indecision also shows that you don't trust your instincts.

10. When we can't follow through on our words, we aren't taking responsibility. It's not as simple as making a promise and not keeping it. You will probably doubt your abilities to follow through and fear letting others down.

11. Negative feelings and emotions need to be processed and let go of. It's often an attachment to the past and the inability to forgive others for their mistakes.

12. It's much easier said than done, but there is no sense in worrying about the future. It steals energy from your present and, with all the potential variables, we can't make accurate predictions.

13. Similarly, worrying about the past isn't going to give us the opportunity to make things right. Everything that happened in the past has provided you with a learning experience. Take the good and don't let the past block your positive thinking.

14. An obsessive need to be right is often associated with an inflated ego. In our case, it's more likely to come from desiring control.

15. Only trusting yourself leads to a very closed life. It's a way of protecting yourself but really, you are still trying to control areas of your life that would be enjoyed more if you were less rigid.

16. One tiny ounce of doubt can develop into stronger negative thoughts. It's hard to trust what others are saying, especially with the amount of fake news we are exposed to. Nevertheless, we need to look at ways to believe what our gut is telling us so that we can believe what others tell us.

17. More often than not, we are burned from previous experiences, and this causes us not to trust others. If there are people in your life who constantly give you reason not to trust them you need to try to distance yourself from them, at least for now. Not being able to trust yourself is often due to focusing on your past mistakes.

18. Having realistic goals is important for our motivation but it can't be the only thing that makes us happy. Be sure to have a clear definition of what makes you happy and what you want to achieve.

19. Judging people is very dangerous as we never truly know what is going on in other people's lives. People have their own difficulties and negative thoughts. Hold yourself to your own standards and let others set their own.

20. Always strive to get what you want. It doesn't make you selfish as long as you aren't hurting others in the process. Just

remember that you can't be too rigid with your goals. It's more important that you are making progress rather than being so determined that you lose sight of the bigger picture.

Intuitive tool #3

It's always important to look at things from a different perspective. For this reason, we are going to look at your levels of positivity. This way, you can look at things with a more all-around understanding of your levels of outlook. After all, as nothing is just black or white, you can use this exercise to create a foundation for your positivity and grow on this.

For the following questions, answer with a number from 1 to 5: 1 is never, 2 rarely, 3 sometimes, 4 usually, 5 always or almost always.

1. If something happens that forces you to change your plan, you look for a positive in the new situation.

2. You like, or at least get on with, the majority of people you deal with/come into contact with.

3. You think that next year will be better than this one.

4. You can take a moment to look around and see the beauty in the world.

5. You can tell the difference between someone giving you feedback and someone just complaining about you or your actions.

6. You say more nice things about friends and family than bad.

7. You believe that the human race will make necessary changes to heal and improve the planet.

8. You are disappointed when someone lets you down or goes back on their word.

9. Overall, you feel that you are happy.

10. You are comfortable being the subject of your own jokes.

11. Your state of mind impacts your physical health.

12. When listing your favorite people, you are one of them.

13. Over the last few months, you have had more successes than setbacks.

Scores over 50 are excellent but even from 45 to 50 you still experience some moments of positive thinking. Once you start looking at numbers below 45 you will find that your negativity is overpowering any positive thoughts you might have. It's very likely that this is the score that you end up with but that's what we would expect at this stage. The goal right now is self-awareness and this list of 13 statements may give you some ideas of positive thinking that you aim to aspire to.

How Do I Know If My Negative Thinking Has Gone beyond a Problem?

One's tolerance for negative thinking will vary. Some people experience negative thinking as something that weighs very heavily on them, but they are still able to carry on with day-to-day tasks.

When negativity starts to affect the ability to make it through the day, this could be a sign of more serious mental health issues. This could include social withdrawal, increased stress, generalized anxiety disorder, depression and/or suicidal thoughts, and obsessive-compulsive disorder.

There are also physical symptoms that can present as a result of continuous negative thinking, such as:

- Headaches

- Chest pain

- Fatigue

- Problems sleeping

- Upset stomach

- Severe changes in metabolism

If you experience any of these emotional or physical symptoms, you should see your doctor as they might recommend therapy. If you are reluctant to see a GP, you can contact confidential support lines such as Supportline or Helpguide.

The techniques that we will look at in the next chapter are backed by science or used by therapists, so it's not that they won't help, it's just that when the problem is so deeply rooted, it helps to talk through your problems.

CHAPTER 3: BEAT NEGATIVE THINKING USING 10 POWERFUL TECHNIQUES

N ow that we have covered the first two letters of L.I.B.E.R.T.Y., learning how our brains work and investigating thought patterns, we are ready to start looking at various techniques for different sets of problems and areas of our lives.

When we talk about the 7 steps of overcoming negativity, this stage is called beating negative thinking.

Changing the Fixed Mindset to a Growth Mindset

The most dangerous thing about a fixed mindset is that it prevents us from trying new things. People convince themselves that they won't be able to do it or that they are going to fail no matter what.

Mistakes are a natural part of life and while we don't want to actively make more mistakes, we can't afford to be so nervous of them that we become stuck in life. When mistakes are made, separate the emotions from the facts, then learn from the facts.

For example, I was stupid to buy that second-hand car without taking it to a mechanic to look over the engine. The emotion is that you feel stupid. There is no evidence of this.

Someone else has sold you a car without disclosing all of the information. The fact is that when buying second-hand cars, it is wise to have it checked by someone who knows their way around a car . The next time you are in the same situation, you will know what to do.

Whether it's a mistake you make or something you see as a failure, use it to your advantage. Once you start practicing mental models like second-order thinking, you will get better at analyzing outcomes and make a plan that will avoid the same mistakes. Accept that this may lead to a setback in your bigger picture, but how much of a setback will depend on your attitude.

To lower the chances of setbacks, you can use the Goldilocks Rule. The Goldilocks Rule states that there is a level of difficulty and challenge that is just right for each person and will encourage optimal levels of motivation.

As the story of Goldilocks goes, one bowl of porridge was too hot, the other was too cold, and the last was just right. Break down all of your tasks so that they are difficult for you but they aren't impossible. Every time you succeed in achieving something that is just right for you, your abilities will improve and so will your confidence.

One amazingly simple trick for adjusting your mindset is to add the word *yet* onto the end of your fixed mindset sentences. A fixed mindset would say "I can't do it." A growth mindset would say "I can't do it yet." It's a tiny but powerful word that reminds you that even though you aren't quite where you want to be, you are working toward it. Another example is if you can't see the solution to a problem, you just can't see the solution yet.

Beware of the two mindsets that can often lead us into problems. The first is the false growth mindset. This is when you think you have a growth mindset but in reality, it's still fixed. You don't just suddenly decide to change the way you view yourself, it takes time. Everybody has moments of fixed and growth mindsets, even the most positive.

While learning and exploring your mindset, focus on what triggers your fixed mindset. This leads to the second problem of an unrecognized fixed mindset which may occur when your subconscious is telling you that you aren't able to do something. During the teenage years, we are predominantly in a fixed mindset as, at this age, we lack the confidence to appreciate what we are capable of. Sometimes as we grow up, this adolescent mindset pops up and tries to influence our current way of thinking.

The growth and fixed mindsets are like a tug of war, fixed is controlled by fear and pulling you toward safety. The growth mindset wants to take you out of your comfort zone and of course, this is scary. Decide where your fears are coming from.

Often, our fears derive from past experiences and, while they might be justifiable, it's worth remembering that you are a different person now. You have learned more about yourself and you are more prepared, reducing the likelihood of the same outcome.

In 1998, studies discovered neuroplasticity, confirming that adult brains are capable of growing new brain cells (Cohen et al., 1998). Furthermore, through repeated actions, the synapses in the brain are strengthened, helping new knowledge become part of our long-term memory. Science tells us that we can increase our abilities and knowledge, now it's a case of believing in yourself.

Put It into Practice

To start the process of developing a growth mindset, here is a list of questions that you can ask yourself:

- What can I learn from this experience?

- What did I learn today? (Make it a goal to learn something new every day.)

- Where can I get more information?

- Where can I get honest, reliable feedback?

- What is the plan to achieve my goal?

- What steps have I taken to achieve my goal?

- Have I made enough effort?

- What can I learn from any mistakes I have made?

- What habit, skill, or knowledge do I need to continue with my plan?

Breaking the Negative Bias Cycle

A quick recap on negativity bias: our brain is wired to be negative. Negative memories are stronger than positive memories, which is why we are better at remembering the bad over the good. Although our brains are wired this way, as we saw in the previous section, we can change this.

The first thing you have to do is decide if the threat/danger/cause of your negativity bias is real. As the Dalai Lama said, if the threat isn't real, there is no point in us worrying and we can move on to strategies that overcome negative thinking. For now, let's look at 4 ways we can break our negativity bias.

1. Watch the movie *Inside Out*

Yes, it's a movie directed at children, but Pixar did the most amazing job at explaining how our memory works. It follows a teenage girl and five characters that represent her emotions: Joy, Fear, Sadness, Anger, and Disgust.

These emotions are in charge of processing and storing memories. The most significant scene for us is when Sadness goes to touch a memory that is related to Joy. Despite Joy's efforts, Sadness affects the memory.

Naturally, Pixar has taken some creative license with science, but the message is true—we can't rely on our memories as our negativity bias causes us to see them in a different way than what actually happened.

When you feel yourself ruminating about the past, immediately stop and find the facts. If you keep a journal, use this over your memory. If other people were involved, ask them.

2. Understand that optimism bias is not the goal

Some people have grown up in an incredibly happy family, they have seen very little hardship and suffering, and they have accomplished everything they have set out to do. Sounds amazing, right? Not necessarily.

Those who have optimism bias take greater risks without always thinking through the consequences. They have no fear of failure, and they might not even see the negatives that are in front of them.

The goal isn't to replace one extreme with the other and it isn't to completely get rid of our negative thinking. In some cases, our negative thoughts can be trying to tell us something. We have to learn how to listen to the thought, find and analyze the facts, and then decide if the negative thought is warranted.

3. Research your idol's mistakes

Our idols are famous for a reason, they have achieved their goals and they are successful. We look at these people in admiration and tell ourselves that we aren't capable of doing the same thing. But every person who has succeeded has gone through their struggles.

For me, it's Colonel Sanders, the founder of KFC. You might assume that he came up with a chicken recipe, opened a restaurant, opened a chain, and got rich. His life is inspiring!

- His father died when he was 5.

- At 13 he dropped out of school, left home, and went to work on a farm.

- His son died at age 20.

- Sanders started various businesses that all failed.

- His café where he began selling chicken in 1939 burned down.

- In 1956, he was unemployed surviving on $105-a-month social security.

- He began teaching restaurants his secret recipe, earning 5¢ for every chicken they sold.

- 7 years later, at the age of 66, he had 600 KFC locations and a year later, sold the franchise for $2 million.

"Do all you can and do it the best you can."

— *COLONEL SANDERS*

Every time Sanders had to close a business, there would have been someone thinking or even telling him that he was stupid, crazy, and didn't have what it took. Regardless of this, he kept going.

People romanticize the lives of their heroes, forgetting that there is a whole side to their lives that we rarely hear about in the news. By looking at your idol and appreciating what they did to get to where they are, you take them off the pedestal and can see them next to you, as a normal human being.

4. Is your body fueling your negativity bias?

Three areas that we have to pay attention to: hunger, tiredness, and alcohol. When faced with a problem, you won't feel the same way about it if you are hungry compared to well-fed.

When we are hungry, blood sugar levels drop and we can become angry, struggle to concentrate, and feel tired. Our coordination suffers, so it's more likely that we drop or break things and make mistakes, all of which will fuel the negativity bias.

When we are tired, it is more difficult to concentrate, and our brains won't be able to engage the mental models that we desperately need.

Despite how we think we feel after a few beers or glasses of wine, alcohol distorts reality and makes it harder to remember things accurately.

If negativity arises when our bodies are not in the best condition, our minds will not be able to function in a neutral or positive way.

Before acting on your negative thoughts, decide whether this is the right time to be taking action or if you should eat, rest, etc. before.

Put It into Practice:

The next time you feel yourself in a situation where your mind or body tells you there is a need to panic but it is just negativity bias (you have assessed that the threat isn't real), take a couple of minutes to listen to your emotions.

I like to imagine this just as the *Inside Out* movie, where each of my emotions is a character. Imagine you are watching a movie about your emotions justifying and explaining their reasoning.

After giving your emotions time to process, look at the situation and find one positive thing. It doesn't have to be huge or life changing.

Let's say you forgot to buy bread, it's so annoying because now you are going to have to go out again or change your meal plans. But there is a positive, why not stop off at a different shop and see if there are new foods that you can try.

Small Differences You Can Make in Your Home to Start Feeling More Positive

Our home can be our sanctuary; that private space where you can close the door to a long day, relax, and start to feel better about yourself. You might be able to close the door to certain things, but your negativity will stick to you like glue.

The majority of the strategies we are looking at focus on changes in the mind and perceptions. Our home can play a large role in how we feel, so here are 6 ways to make your home more positive according to scientists.

- Let in as much natural light as possible. Natural light comes from the sun, our favorite source of vitamin D. The body produces more vitamin D when exposed to sunshine. Vitamin D can reduce the chances of catching the flu (American Journal of Clinical Nutrition, 2010). It can reduce the symptoms of anxiety and depression and lower the risk of heart disease (Circulation, 2008).

- Have a good clear-out, donating, recycling, and selling what you don't need. Clutter in the home can increase stress. Don't feel you have to do the entire house in one go, just make it a mission to do it bit-by-bit.

- Buy a plant. Plants bring a sense of nature into your home. The color green is well-known for having a calming effect, but plants can do more than help you relax. They can improve air quality, reducing CO_2 and increasing levels of oxygen which improves concentration and productivity. Interestingly, since 2019, some doctors in the U.K. have been prescribing house plants to patients with anxiety, depression, or loneliness (Manchester City Council, 2019).

- Paint your home. Again, it doesn't all have to be done at once, but think about starting in the main living space where you spend most of your time. For those who are not comfortable reinventing themselves, freshening up the walls is a great way to start a makeover and it doesn't have to cost a lot. You can marvel at your efforts, especially if you have never painted a room before.

- Add color with art and decorations. Certain colors have been proven to improve people's moods and often without them even realizing it as each color has a specific wavelength and particular energy.

Warm colors like yellow and orange are mood-lifters. Blue can also have an excellent impact on your mood, contrary to the expression "feeling blue." When blue lights were installed in 71 Japanese train stations, there was an 84% decrease in suicides from people jumping in front of trains (Matsubayashi et al., 2012).

Make sure you choose the warmer shades of colors. For example, dark blue can have a heavy, depressing feel to it. Warmer tones of orange can help you feel positive whereas bright orange brings about excitement, which might make it difficult to relax.

• Experiment with essential oils. Twelve studies published by the National Center for Biotechnology Information in 2017 showed that aromatherapy improved depressive symptoms. Some of the best essential oils to improve your mood include rosemary, sweet orange, jasmine, ylang-ylang, and lavender. Of course, if the smell of lavender irritates you, it's not going to help, which is why it is worth trying different scents to see their effects.

Making some or all of these small changes isn't going to just stop the negative thought patterns. They are tips that will create a more positive environment for you.

In a positive environment, you will find it easier to look for more optimistic solutions and alternatives and it can make you feel that little bit stronger and more able to handle your situation.

Put It into Practice

No excuses, this week you need to take three tiny steps to a more positive home. For less than $10, you can get a house plant and one essential oil.

Task number three, declutter just one area. It could be a drawer or a cupboard, there is no need to set your hopes on decluttering an entire room.

These three goals are easy to achieve, so you will feel better about yourself quickly. Then just take a few days to see if you notice a difference with the plant and essential oil. Next week, get another plant and another essential oil. Keep track of how these little changes make you feel.

Beat Negative Thoughts That Arise at Inappropriate Times

In a perfect world, our negative thoughts would come up at a time when we could sit down and work our way through the emotion. But, as we can't control when the mind takes over, it's more than likely that you have had negative thoughts that led to anxiety and possibly even panic attacks at the most inappropriate times.

During our day, there are moments when we can't afford to break down. We could be driving our cars and not be paying attention to the road. It might be during a meeting or presentation, or perhaps when your children need you.

In these moments we need to be at the top of our game, which means that we need to beat negative thoughts but not forget them. It's a pause so that we can finish the task at hand and then take the time to understand why the negative thought appeared and what can be done about it. To stop something in an instant, you and your brain have to act pretty quickly. It's a matter of seconds, but don't worry, the brain is perfectly capable of working at such speeds.

Visual imagery can work wonders to block a negative thought. You could imagine a stop sign, the edge of a cliff, or even a positive image like your favorite ice cream, a good-looking actor—think about an image that makes you stop in your tracks.

Once the brakes are on, take a deep breath. It sounds like a cliché but diaphragmatic breathing, or deep breathing, lowers cortisol levels, decreasing the stress we experience. Body image has caused some people to change the way they naturally breathe. By holding stomachs in to encourage a flat stomach, we prevent the bottom part of our lungs from filling with air. This chest breathing can increase anxiety.

Put It into Practice

Take a breath now, not forced but normal. Pay attention to the number of seconds you inhale for and the number of seconds you exhale for.

Now, take another breath but now deeper, imagine the oxygen filling up every inch of your lungs like a balloon.

There is a 4-7-8 rule for deep breathing. Inhale for 4 seconds, hold for 7 and exhale for 8. The actual number of seconds is not the most important part; you should make sure that you exhale for longer than you inhale.

Being aware of how deep your breathing can be will help you to correctly deep breath when blocking a negative thought.

If you practice deep breathing on a regular basis, you can also lower your blood pressure, get a better night's sleep, and improve your concentration (WebMD, 2021).

Another technique to stop negative thinking in the moment is to practice aversion therapy tricks.

Keep an elastic band on your wrist. When a negative thought appears, flick the rubber band. Your subconscious learns that there is an association between negative thinking and the pain of the elastic band.

There are studies that show positive results and others that contradict the practice. At the very least, it will provide a distraction from the original negative thought.

Take a moment to pause and think about the emotional characters in your brain. Detach yourself from the critical voice you hear so that you can see your emotions for what they really are.

You can try adding a sentence like "I am having this thought that…" and add what you are thinking. It doesn't sound like a huge difference, but this separates your negative thoughts from you as a person because it's not the same as "I think…"

Finally, take control and responsibility. There is a split second between where we can successfully block the thought and when the thought can spiral out of control.

It is difficult and, in these situations, it's important to be hard on yourself rather than feel like you are the victim. You can control what happens next.

You decide if you continue with the activity that needs your attention, or if you continue with your negative thoughts. Hold yourself accountable for what happens next!

Thinking Your Way to Positivity

The ability to think positively is going to help you manage stress, increase your energy levels, and lower the symptoms of depression. One extensive study looked at 70,000 women between 2004 and 2012. It showed that those who were optimistic were less at risk of heart disease, stroke, several types of cancer, infections, and respiratory diseases (American Journal of Epidemiology, 2017).

Positivity doesn't just happen. We need to make it happen and sometimes, this is going to take effort on your part. There is always something positive if we look hard enough. It might not be obvious, and you may need some time to see it, but it will be there.

If you get stood up on a date, it's hard to see anything good. But the truth is, you have just saved yourself months of dating someone who was never going to be good enough for you. It's pouring down with rain and you have a million errands to run. Well, there is nothing better than sitting by the window with a hot drink and watching the rain once you have finished all you have to do.

On a similar note, being grateful for what we have boosts positivity, well-being, and mental health. 300 college students were separated into three groups. One group wrote a gratitude letter to another student each week for 12 weeks. Another group wrote down their negative thoughts and feelings while the third group didn't write anything.

The results showed that not only did those who wrote gratitude letters feel better, they also experienced fewer toxic emotions (Wong et al., 2016). The same study also discovered that you didn't actually need to share the letter with anyone to experience the benefits.

To kick-start positive thinking, it's a great idea to surround yourself with positive people. Positivity is like a snowball at the top of a mountain. It picks up momentum and grows with every turn. It's magnetic; a force you can't escape and should never want to.

Positive people have an abundance of energy, and it rubs off onto others without draining their own levels. Imagine the time you spend with positive people as an opportunity to recharge your battery. Notice the vocabulary they use and that even the speed at which they speak is energetic.

Positive people are often very funny and good at making people laugh. Don't feel that you have to be the source of laughter, but you can appreciate humor and its benefits. Laughing releases endorphins, which encourage an overall feel-good feeling. It might not be a full-on belly laugh straight away, but more smiling is a good start.

It's an uphill battle when you are putting all the work into thinking more positively, but then you turn on the news and everything is negative.

It's not to say that you can never watch the news again, just be careful about how much negativity you expose yourself to.

If you are feeling down, now is not the time to let more negativity in. If you are feeling positive, maybe just hold onto that feeling for a little longer. The news will still be there later.

I find it helpful to have a news app. This way, I can scroll through the headlines and choose what I want to read or watch. This is a good way to still keep up on what's happening in the world without going into all of the details that can drag you down.

Put It into Practice

Put down the book or the tablet and look around for one positive thing. It's strange what positivity means to different people. It could be that your favorite series is next on TV, the second chin you had seems to be a little smaller, or your windows don't need cleaning for another few weeks!

On a bigger scale, your mom might nag you about your personal life, but she still makes you your favorite meal every time you visit. Your coworker is annoying, but you have a steady paycheck at the end of each month!

Now, start every day doing the same thing. Find one positive and hold on to that thought for the day. After just a few days, it starts getting easier.

Next, create a new folder on your phone, tablet, or computer. Do a quick internet search on memes and GIFs to make you laugh. Scroll through and choose 5 to 10 that genuinely make you laugh and don't worry if they are stupid or not to everyone's humor, it's only for you. Save your memes and GIFs in the new folder. During your morning tea or coffee, have a quick look through them. Delete them when they get old, add new ones, but each morning, start the day with a laugh.

Talking Your Way to Positivity

"You live the words you tell yourself in your mind."

— DR. MAGDALENA BATTLES

For some reason, talking to yourself is a sign of craziness yet negative self-talk is perfectly acceptable. We need to put a stop to any form of critical thinking toward ourselves. Self-talk is the messages and opinions that you are telling yourself. It could be related to your abilities, knowledge, or how you did on a particular activity.

Negative self-talk is closely related to a fixed mindset. It's the voice inside us that tells us we can't do things, or that we will never be able to. There is often a lot of "what ifs" and "if onlys" with negative self-talk.

For example, "If only I hadn't made that stupid comment" or "I wish I hadn't agreed to do this." What we tell ourselves will have a massive impact on the next decisions we make. It determines whether or not we keep trying.

Imagine you want to start your own blog. You have written a couple of articles, but nobody is interacting. Negative self-talk tells you that you aren't a good writer, and you have nothing interesting to share with others.

On the other hand, positive self-talk tells you that you need to work on your advertising. In one scenario, you give up. In the other, you try again and succeed. If you pay attention to negative self-talk, you will never feel the joy of success.

Continuous negative self-talk is going to drain you of your confidence and may even create distance between you and others. Because of the fear negative self-talk instills, we start to feel as if we are paralyzed, stuck in this situation with no way forward.

Learning to choose positive self-talk is a more challenging topic, so in Chapter 7 we will go into greater detail. Nevertheless, here are a few tips on how to start generating more positive self-talk.

Pay close attention to your words. It often becomes so natural that you don't notice how much negative vocabulary you use.

Typical negative words include no, not, never, nothing, and nobody. Then you have all of the negative contractions like can't and shouldn't.

The killer negative word is "but." When you end a sentence with but, it often precedes an excuse. "I could go to the gym but there is going to be traffic." Later, the excuse leads to more negative talk because we feel fat and unattractive.

Stop comparing yourself to others. It only causes negative self-talk and how we view other people is often very distorted. If someone gets a promotion over you, it's not because they are better than you.

They may have had to make great sacrifices to get there or taken extra courses and improved their skills. A friend who is always entertaining the crowd isn't more amazing than you are, they just have more confidence.

Put It into Practice

We are going to work in threes for now. Remember there will be more on positive self-talk later but, for now, let's practice eliminating some negative self-talk.

Spend a day taking note of the negative vocabulary you use. You don't need to go to the extent of writing a list, unless you want to. Decide which three words you most frequently use and ban yourself from using them. Take the old swear jar system and turn it into your negative jar!

Now, take three beliefs you have about yourself. In your journal or a piece of paper, change these beliefs so that they portray a growth mindset. For example:

#1. I'm never going to find the right person.

I'm not ready for the right person in my life yet.

#2. I can't complete a sudoku.

I will learn how to complete a sudoku this month.

#3. I'm stuck in this job forever.

Once I have gained more confidence, I will look for a new job.

Not all but sentences are negative. We are going to use the reverse but to take away any negative implications. Instead of saying "I want to go to the gym but there is going to be traffic." reverse it. "There is going to be traffic, but I want to go to the gym." The traffic is no longer an excuse, it's an acceptance. The next time you feel a "but" coming, reverse it.

How to Overcome Automatic Negative Thinking

By definition, these types of thoughts are very difficult to stop. They pop up unexpectedly and we have little to no control over them. As we can't prevent them, it's critical that we learn how to deal with them. Don't worry though, your automatic negative thinking will slow down once you start to see improvements in your outlook.

The first thing you need to do is attack the automatic negative thoughts head-on. To do this, detach yourself from the thought, give it a little *Inside Out* persona and question it. Ask this persona if they are based on fact or opinion and if there is any advice to back up its presence. Have they appeared to help you or hinder you?

If you struggle to detach yourself from the automatic thought, write it down. It sounds too simple but writing it down provides a space between you and the thought. It gives you a visual to use rather than letting the thought spin around in your head.

Keeping track of your thoughts on paper is another way to understand what types of thoughts are occurring. Many times, we are weighed down by so much negative thinking but if you go back and look at what you have written down, they tend to be based around the same idea. All of a sudden, 100 automatic negative thoughts can be narrowed down to 10.

How many times have you listened to someone tell the same story over and over again but they seem to forget you have already heard it? In your mind, you can't stop thinking about how boring this story is, but you are too polite to say anything. Your automatic negative thought doesn't have feelings. It won't be offended or angry if you turn around and say "Listen, I've heard this a dozen times and you're boring me."

You can also imagine your negative thought as a persona in an empty room with just a light bulb. Be the person to grab the cord and turn the light off. Perhaps the persona is on a boat sailing away and Andrea Bocelli is singing "Time to Say Goodbye."

The point of these visual exercises is that your mind is more focused on removing the persona than it is on what the negative thought actually is.

Automatic negative thoughts can also be greatly reduced by changing the vocabulary we use. Should and shouldn't bring about negativity because they are putting pressure on you that you may not be able to handle at the time.

Think of the sentence "I should save for my retirement." This is sensible and true, but what if you haven't paid your car off yet, or you haven't secured a mortgage. The financial pressure starts to mount but there is no plan for how you can achieve your goals.

Rather than emphasizing what you should do, create a sentence that reminds you of what you want to achieve but creates action instead of pressure. "When I get a mortgage, I'm going to set up a separate fund for my retirement."

Put It into Practice

Today, you are going to be an Agony Aunt (or Uncle). Your automatic negative thought has been personified into a friend and they are telling you what is wrong. Your friend says "I am never going to be able to stop smoking." Remember, you aren't giving yourself advice, you are dealing with a friend. What would you tell them?

Regardless of what negative thought your "friend" comes up with, look for objective ways to overcome their issue. It's amazing how easy it is to tell others what to do but ignore the advice ourselves. When you offer guidance to someone else, you get the chance to see how wise and empathic you really are.

4 Methods to Stop Negative Spiraling

According to Dr. Fred Luskin of Stanford University, 90% of our thoughts throughout the day are repeated. We already know that most of our thoughts are negative, but now consider how many of our negative thoughts each day are on a repetitive loop.

There is a serious problem with this. First, that is an awful lot of mental noise that we take everywhere with us. Aside from making it more difficult to think positively, there is very little chance of gaining mental peace.

What's more, the opportunity for one thought to spiral out of control is increased. This can have a tornado effect. It may start off small but as it scoops up more thoughts in its path, it becomes a catastrophe.

Another way to look at it is as downward spiraling negative thoughts. Much like a rock starts off slowly rolling down a hill, it quickly picks up momentum as it gets further down the hill.

Let's take an example of working fewer hours this month and earning less than usual. You can make the mortgage payment, but you won't be able to make the car payment. If the same thing happens the following month, you will then be two months behind and risk losing your car. Without the car, you can't get to work and risk losing your job. The downward spiral continues as now you face losing your home.

Negative downward spirals can occur with even the smallest negative thought. Maybe you rushed out the door and forgot to empty the washing machine. Now when you go home, you are going to have to redo the laundry as well as wash the dishes you didn't have time to do. The kids have their activities, and you were supposed to help a friend run through their work proposal.

As the rock starts to speed up, we become suffocated by all of the other things that need to be done, even those that don't necessarily have to be done today.

The real danger comes when we can't control these spiraling thoughts and they lead to panic attacks. You may have already noticed other negative health impacts such as insomnia, unhealthy habits relating to diet and exercise, or greater levels of stress and depression.

Many of the previous strategies will help to reduce negative thoughts spiraling. You don't want to try to block the thoughts or try to replace them with positive ones. Assess whether the thought is justified or if there is evidence behind it. The trick now is to act before there is a chance for it to get out of control.

To do this, visualize your spiral of negative thoughts. Start at the bottom and unravel it until you get to the very first original thought. Accept that this original thought is an automatic thought, but you do have control of the thoughts that follow. To stop the spiral beginning again, we need to flip the coin to see the other side of the original thought.

If you have worked fewer hours and you fear the same will happen next month, what can you do about this? You could take advantage of the free time and declutter your home, selling all that you don't need. You could sign up to freelancing websites and pick up some small jobs to tide you over.

If your home is a mess, accept it. Yes, it's a negative, but by allowing the spiral to take control, you will affect your energy levels and motivation, so when you get home, you will be too exhausted to do anything.

Focus on doing something constructive like a to-do list to help clear your mind. Organize all you have to do by priority and attach a reward to each activity so that you are feeding your brain with positive thoughts to go with each negative.

Each time you feel the initial negative thought pop into your mind, remind yourself of the flip side. "I'm not going to earn as much from my job but I'm excited about clearing out my kitchen." "When I finish the two jobs I didn't do this morning, I can get out of my work clothes and get comfy."

We aren't fighting the negative thought by replacing it with a negative. Instead, we are recognizing that the thought is there and accompanying it with a positive.

Put It into Practice

One of the quickest ways to do this is to change your environment. If you are sitting in your kitchen and the spiraling begins, walk away. Step outside, go to your bedroom.

By changing your surroundings, you are giving your brain more to take in. It can remind you of something that you need to do that will occupy your brain.

If you can't change your environment, change your activity. Even if it is just from checking accounts to responding to emails. The brain needs new stimuli to defer the thought from taking control.

The second technique is brain dumping, an awesome method to stop the spiraling. Take a pen and paper and set a timer for 15 minutes. During this time, you need to write absolutely everything negative on your mind, significant or insignificant.

There is no need to question the legitimacy right now because the clock is ticking. When the timer runs out, you should be free of negative thoughts. For a brain dump to work, you need to destroy the paper. Burn it, flush it, shred it—just don't keep it.

The third method is another visualization tip. When negative thoughts start to spiral out of control, it might be helpful for you to remember and visualize how the brain works.

Don't worry about all the technical terms for the brain. I picture my brain as a balloon with blobs of blue and blobs of red. The blue are my negative thoughts and the red, positive.

All these blobs are bouncing around coming into contact with each other. When the blue blobs come together, they become stronger, taking over all of the space. My job is defense. Each time I feel these negative blue blobs coming together, I need to place a red one in between.

The fourth technique is to imagine your negative thoughts as the news ticker or crawler. This is the text that comes up at the bottom/top of the screen while you are watching other stories. It's a constant reel of text with very brief spaces. Treat these as pauses in your negative thinking. This technique allows the negative thoughts to exist rather than ignoring them, but it gives your mind moments of peace while you are focused on the pause. Each time the pause comes around, make it a little longer.

Essential Tips to Remove Toxic Thoughts

Toxic thoughts are the extreme of negative thinking. They are vicious and can seriously increase stress and anxiety. Toxic thoughts could be about ourselves, but they can also be about others.

When a driver makes a mistake in front of you, do you let it slide, or are you raging at them in your head? Raging is toxic!

There are various reasons for our toxic thoughts:

• We personalize our failures (I'm not good enough).

• We fear rejection (They won't love me if...).

• We expect perfection (It should have been better).

• We see ourselves as the victim (This is just my luck).

• We blame others (If they had arrived on time, none of this would have happened).

• We don't appreciate the true meaning of happiness (If I had more money...).

• We feel the need to justify our bad behavior (I had to do it because...).

If the toxic thoughts are about yourself or your abilities, you need to go back and determine if they are warranted. If you are worried about how others will feel because of your reactions, consider whether their opinion holds more value than your own happiness.

There are toxic people in the world whose opinions shouldn't affect you at all. Their hurtful sentences aren't based on truth but only a tool for them to get what they want. It's essential that you distance yourself from anyone who provokes toxic thoughts. At least steer clear of them until you are strong enough to deal with toxic people.

You are not a bad person and it's perfectly normal to fall victim to envy. Still, you can't allow toxic thoughts to make you the victim. The grass isn't greener on the other side. The grass is greener where you water it.

If someone has a quality or material object that you want, there is no rule that says you can't have the same. Where you are now isn't because of bad luck or destiny. There is a positive alternative to choose if you want to.

While on the subject of grass, I often look at my neighbor's garden and envy their flowers. I wanted to be able to grow strawberries to eat and pick my own herbs. It made me bitter and slightly resentful toward them. It wasn't their fault that I didn't have the skill and they weren't stopping me from learning.

I swallowed my pride and asked for their advice. Not only were they more than happy to share their gardening tips, but we also have a great relationship now, improving my social life outside of work and family.

Put It into Practice

This practice is all about overcoming toxic thoughts with kindness. It's a daily practice. First, find the good in someone. When someone says something that causes you to think in a toxic way, look for the good in them. For example, if someone offers your constructive criticism, your first thought may be to take this as a negative attack. Rethink what they have said and think about how they were really trying to help you.

Each day, say something nice to someone. Pay them a compliment. Again, you need to first find the good in that person so that your kind words are genuine. In a world where people are toxic to each other before they are nice, you are setting a great example of how things should be. Soon, people will catch on and start returning the kind words.

Finally, every day, take a moment to be generous. This doesn't have to cost you a lot of money. Be generous with your time or your food. If you see someone having a worse day than you, buy them a coffee and appreciate their smile.

The more good you can do, the better you will feel about yourself, and the easier it will be to discard toxic thoughts that have no evidence.

Coping with Returning Negative Thoughts

Negative thoughts that keep returning can be a combination of the previously mentioned. They could be toxic thoughts caused by other people's behavior or your own. They might start off small but grow as you ruminate more. You might have identified an automatic negative thought that keeps reappearing.

Whatever the trigger for these thoughts that keep cropping up, you have to remember that changing the way you think is going to take time. As with any mental health issue, you need to put in the time and effort for the results to show.

This is going to require patience and, above all, compassion toward yourself. You have probably felt like your negativity has taken over to the extent that you feel you don't deserve to take care of and spoil yourself. We are going to look at self-care further on in the book. Keep making little differences to your home so that you are creating a more positive environment.

Constantly question where these negative thoughts are coming from. And, for those persistent thoughts that just don't give up, personify them and let them know that you are tired of the same story.

If you haven't already, now is the time to start a journal. Because the progress is ongoing, it is extremely beneficial to spend 10 to 15 minutes each day writing down how you feel. This gives you time to process your thoughts and feelings and analyze which are distorted. Many people turn to journaling when they don't feel comfortable talking to others about how they feel.

Put It into Practice

For now, make a note of all the things you do in a week that go toward your own health and well-being. What positive things are you doing? Do you walk to work instead of taking the car? Are you getting enough sleep and time to yourself? What about your diet, do you think it's well-balanced?

In order to keep going on your journey to a positive outlook, you need to have inner strength. Take this time to figure out how you are boosting your inner strength.

You now have an arsenal of tools that will enable you to take control of all different types of negative thinking. Not all of them are going to work for you because we all have such different personalities. Don't discount them without giving yourself time to appreciate the difference. Keep track of how much of a difference each method makes.

The next chapter is going to focus on rumination. What keeps us up at night and blocks us from living in the present. With the information and practice exercises, you will be able to develop better decision-making skills and make those choices that lead you to a better life.

CHAPTER 4: ELIMINATE RUMINATION AND OVERTHINKING IN JUST A FEW EASY WAYS

W e have already discussed the difference between negative thoughts and rumination. While rumination may involve negative thoughts, it's more of a constant nagging feeling rather than a suffocating feeling.

Many people feel that ruminating leaves them spending too much time thinking about their past and future, a ditch that they are stuck in that prevents them from living in the present. There is no off button and people often find themselves up all night with these extremely intrusive thoughts.

In most cases, we are able to put some space between ourselves and rumination, but that doesn't stop the problem as we only beat ourselves up for overthinking and worrying.

We have to make an effort to stop rumination so that our pasts and futures don't define who we are in this moment. By doing so, we are able to live with more clarity and a better understanding of our circumstances.

Let's take a look at a real-life example of negative thinking and rumination.

Paul split up with his girlfriend about 6 months ago. She said some pretty harsh things about both his physical appearance and his personality.

His negative thinking caused him to replay these words over and over again. He believed he was a bad person and that his ex was completely right. He was a walkover, he had no backbone, and he had put on weight in their time together.

His rumination caused him to think about how he should have started playing football with his friends to control his weight. He thought about the future and how he was never going to have the confidence to meet another woman at his age.

He wanted to change his personality so that more people would like him. The changes he wanted to make overwhelmed him to the extent that he couldn't do anything about it.

Paul has to work on his negative thinking because the only thing his girlfriend had said that was based on evidence was the slight weight gain.

While the previous chapter can help him overcome negative thought patterns, this chapter will overcome the continuous hum of rumination.

7 Ways to Combat Rumination and Overthinking

When rumination starts, you need to put a stop to it as quickly as possible. This way you can prevent it from spiraling out of control and leading to even darker thoughts.

As with many of our thought processes, the first step is to understand our triggers. What is it that has caused rumination to begin? Were you doing a particular activity or with a certain person?

Examples:

• Visiting a city you went to on holiday with your ex is going to stir up memories.

• Spending time with a toxic person may lead you to question how you aren't spending your time wisely.

• Cooking the same meals as your grandma who passed away will stir up feelings of loss and mourning.

• Watching a particular movie might bring up emotions related to your own experiences.

It's not to say that you won't ever be able to do these things again. It just means that before you revisit these triggers, you need to take control of your overthinking. Here is how!

1. Find a distraction

Many people find that rumination starts when the mind is at a loss for something to do. If you are focused on an activity, your mind is too busy to think of something else.

As soon as you spot the first signs of overthinking, get up and do something different. Go for a walk, do some cleaning, or read a book.

For these times, I highly recommend brain training apps and puzzles on your phone. Not only do you stop rumination, but you also give your brain a positive workout.

2. Talk to people

Sometimes, just a phone call to a friend or family member is enough to distract the brain. You don't need to discuss what is worrying you, especially if you are worried about how others feel about your constant worrying.

On the other hand, if you approach the subject in a way that doesn't come across as just complaining about your life, you can gain some amazing insights.

Rather than telling people what you are worrying about, let them know that you are worrying and ask for their advice on how you can overcome this.

People are much more inclined to lend you their ear when you want to do something about it instead of just complaining. You don't necessarily need to take their advice, but definitely consider it.

3. Make a plan

Rumination is often a trick our brain plays on us to think we are coming up with solutions when really, we are just stuck.

Define the problem that is causing your worrying in one sentence. Then start working backward through each step so that you have an actionable plan to resolve the issue.

Don't forget that each step must be small and manageable.

4. Don't wait to take action

I always advise people to make the first step on their action plan something that they can do straight away. If your plan begins with "talk to X about Y," you will do this the next time you see them. It gets the ball rolling.

If you are worried about your health and want to start eating more fruits and vegetables, don't wait till the shops are open. The first step of your action plan should be to find 3 new healthy recipes, which you can do straight away.

5. Question your overthinking

Just like with our negative thoughts, it's essential to decide if the cause of your rumination is justifiable.

Do you genuinely have a problem that you can solve or is the source of your worrying in someone else's hands? Are you losing sleep over a presentation, but your coworker is preparing the materials and you only have to show up? Is it possible that you have lost perspective and a molehill has now become a mountain?

Question your thoughts and challenge them.

6. Reassess your goals

Having goals is an important help to achieve our desires. Without goals it's easy to remain in this ditch with no movement. Sometimes, we set unachievable goals, and this causes us to dwell on how we are going to reach them instead of creating the plan to get there. We also have to be careful that our goals don't require perfectionism.

Isn't it better to first learn how to restore furniture and then work on perfecting your technique? Shouldn't you aim to run a half-marathon before a marathon? You can perfect a skill, with time. But if your goal is to get it perfect the first time, the act of starting will be even more daunting.

7. Give your self-esteem a boost

People who think poorly of themselves are more inclined to ruminate. Both rumination and low self-esteem can be linked to a greater risk of depression.

We are all good at something when we look hard enough. It can be something small like finishing a crossword in record time, bringing plants back from the dead, or cooking restaurant-quality desserts.

Don't feel you have to show your skills off to the world, but take time to enjoy these activities and build on them as well as learning new skills.

Next, we will take a closer look at some different types of rumination and how to overcome them, starting with how we can stop the past from interrupting our present and falsely predicting our future.

Learning How to Not Let the Past and Future Dictate Your Present

According to a study by psychologists Matthew Killingsworth and Daniel Gilbert, we spend 46.9% of our waking day thinking about something other than the task we are doing. That's nearly 47% of our time thinking about the past, the future, or events that may not even happen.

Our days are full of events, some appear meaningless and mundane like driving to work. Others are once-in-a-lifetime opportunities, creating memories with our children, parents, or friends. When we are unable to enjoy the present, our mind takes over and robs us of these special moments.

True, driving to work isn't exactly special, but we could find a way to enjoy it rather than overthinking. Why is it that we take time to create a delicious meal, but then eat it in a matter of minutes because there are other things to do?

We are stealing these small joys in life by worrying about what has happened or what is to come.

Rumination about the past

Like all types of overthinking, you want to knock this one on the head as soon as you realize your mind has started to think about the past. Do this by changing your activity to jolt your brain into a different thought.

We aren't going to just ignore the thought because it will keep coming back. We are going to schedule a time to deal with it.

When you are in the right frame of mind, often after exercising or achieving a small goal, readdress the past thought. To start with, you are now in control because it's not an automatic thought that has just popped up.

Rewrite the past event but with a more balanced and objective ending. You aren't going to change the result, but this will give you an opportunity to see both the good and the bad.

Imagine you had an argument with your parents, and you are still replaying what was said on both sides. Currently, you are still angry and upset and this might be influencing the way you are thinking and that it is all bad.

However, even though you could have phrased things in a more constructive way, you still managed to tell your parents the things they needed to hear.

Looking at it from a new perspective, you might see that while you should apologize for the way you spoke, you have a chance to reiterate what had been annoying you. The end result will be another conversation with your parents and a stronger relationship.

Rumination about the future

This is what we have characterized as mind-reading or fortune-telling. Regardless of what is most likely to happen, negative bias and past experiences cause our minds to jump straight to the worst-case scenario.

The absolute classic example of this is "We need to talk!" If it's your partner, you're getting dumped. If it's your child, they are dropping out of school. If it's your parents, they are dying. If it's your boss, you're getting fired. No one has ever heard the words "We need to talk" and thought they were getting a pay raise! The brain just isn't wired that way.

Still, this constant fear of what is going to happen in the future, known as anticipatory anxiety, can prevent us from concentrating. It can also impact our emotions and our ability to manage them. Physically, we can get jumpy or experience tension in our bodies. If this goes on for a long period of time, it's normal to have problems eating, sleeping, and going about our daily lives.

Anticipatory anxiety can be a symptom of social anxiety, phobias, PTSD, and panic disorders. In these cases, you might need professional help to get to the source of the anxiety, especially if it has developed into a fear that stops you from doing things (i.e., a fear of dogs stops you from going to any park and the sight of a dog causes a panic attack).

The most important way to overcome rumination about the future is to take care of your physical self. The connection between the body and the mind is extremely powerful and having a healthy body eases the strain on the mind. Creating a routine that includes a balanced diet, exercise, and enough time to get the necessary sleep is a great start.

You can also cut down on caffeine and sugar that tends to make people a little jittery. You can replace these habits with relaxation techniques to further relax the mind and body. There will be lots more on this later on!

Techniques to Stop Rumination for a Better Night's Sleep

They say never go to bed on a full stomach, but what is equally helpful is never to go to bed with a full mind!

Bedtime is one of the worst times for rumination. There are no distractions and the silence seems to fuel our thinking.

Before looking at what you can do, take a moment to consider what you should avoid doing.

As previously mentioned, caffeine isn't going to help you. Sadly, you should give up the afternoon coffee.

For the best chances of falling asleep, you need to try and give up caffeine after 3 p.m.

Exercise is going to help but again, you need to choose the right time. Avoid aerobic exercise at least 90 minutes before you go to bed, or you will still be feeling the energy from the workout and it will impact your sleep cycle.

Be careful how late you work into the night.

Today, it seems perfectly normal to be working at home in the evenings, even answering messages and emails up to the point of going to bed.

You might feel like you are being productive and there is less to do in the morning, but the opposite occurs.

If there isn't enough time between switching off from work and going to bed, you are going to take it with you.

You may also think that taking your phone to bed or watching a series on the tablet helps to distract your mind and makes it easier to fall asleep. Science tells us otherwise.

All electronic devices emit blue light. This blue light has a short wavelength, which delays the production of melatonin, the hormone that makes us feel sleepy.

Not only do you want to avoid technology in the bedroom, but you should also look at changing bright light bulbs to warm colors that are more relaxing.

Creating a perfect routine to eliminate nighttime rumination

The perfect bedtime routine is going to vary from person to person. If possible, try to incorporate as many of these ideas as possible.

• Set a shut-off time for work. Ideally, this will be at least an hour before going to bed. It will be hard to stick to this new rule at first but once you start getting more sleep, you will have more energy to achieve more throughout the day and it will be easier to say no to late-night jobs.

• Write your to-do list for the following day. Oftentimes, our brains go over all that we have to do the next day, worried about what we are forgetting. Take 10 minutes to seriously think about what needs to be done the next day and list these things in order of priority. Walk away and do another activity and then revisit your list in case there is anything missing. After a second check, leave it for the next day.

• Write in your journal. Like brain dumping the to-do list, writing in your journal gives you a chance to process thoughts and concerns rather than taking them to bed with you. End your journal entry with a few things that you are grateful for or some positive statements.

• Do something that is relaxing and makes you feel good. This could be meditation, having a warm drink, or a relaxing bath or shower. This can be 10 to 20 minutes of time just for you, a treat that you deserve after a long day. This can include face masks, preparing the next day's smoothie, or listening to your favorite vinyl—just a little time for self-care.

• When in bed, begin with progressive muscle relaxation. Tense your toes, breathe in, and hold for 5 seconds. Slowly exhale as you release the tension. Next, do the same for your calf muscles, and then your thighs. Work your way up until all of the tension is released.

• Read a book. A mattress review site asked 1,000 people about their sleep routine. Those who read slept for an average of 1 hour and 37 minutes more than those who didn't. Reading is an all-around healthy habit that can reduce stress, encourage empathy, and expand your vocabulary.

• Certain essential oils have been proven to promote a good night's sleep. Lavender calms the nervous system. The combination of bergamot and sandalwood improved the quality of sleep in 64% of participants in one study (Dyer et al., 2016). Clary sage oil reduces cortisol levels, which negatively impact our sleep cycles (Lee et al., 2014).

• Finally, if you can't fall asleep and you find worrying thoughts stirring, repeat another round of progressive muscle relaxation and pick your book up again. If this doesn't have the right effect, get up before overthinking takes over. Take 20 minutes to do another activity before trying to go back to bed. This activity should be boring so that you aren't rewarding your brain. Try folding laundry or cleaning the toilet!

Don't give up on your bedtime routine. It can take anywhere from 18 to 254 days for a new routine to become a habit (European Journal of Social Psychology, 2009).

That doesn't mean it will take this long to see the benefits. And you may want to adjust small parts of your routine so that it is more effective. It's not an overnight fix but instead small, effective steps that will last a lifetime.

Coping with Unwanted Intrusive Thoughts

Intrusive thoughts are a type of negative thought. They are involuntary patterns of images or thoughts that are upsetting and may lead to depression. The images and thoughts are so strong that people can become obsessed with them. Intrusive thoughts are closely linked to OCD and substance abuse.

Intrusive thoughts are very much a part of everyday life. A study by Concordia University found that 94% of people experience these thoughts. We do, however, need to take control of these types of thoughts before they manifest into obsessive thoughts or more severe mental health problems.

Intrusive thoughts can be things like a fear that you are going to catch an illness or disease, which has been extremely common since the coronavirus outbreak. They might be images of breaking the law, hurting someone, or inappropriate thoughts or images of sex.

A married person might think about having an affair, a flash of an image if they see someone they have a crush on. When they can't get this thought out of their mind and it starts affecting their relationship, it has become an obsessive thought and possibly an underlying sign of OCD.

When somebody is suffering from intrusive thoughts of OCD, the fear will be very specific to them. Most of us at some point have worried about coronavirus, but only intrusive thoughts of OCD would focus on a specific fear like being killed in a car accident or a family member dying. The emotional distress this person feels can be indescribable, especially when they are so detailed. OCD intrusive thoughts can develop into severe social anxiety.

Like negative thinking and rumination, intrusive thoughts can be linked to depression. Furthermore, more than 25% of patients with OCD meet the criteria for a substance abuse disorder (Journal of Anxiety Disorders, 2008).

If you feel like your intrusive thoughts are out of control and they have developed into a more serious condition, it's a good idea to get professional help. Cognitive-behavioral therapy has been very successful in the treatment of obsessive thoughts.

How to conquer intrusive thoughts

1. Gain clear insight into your core values

The first step is to understand why these intrusive thoughts are causing you so much upset. The reason might be a trigger.

Unfortunately, if someone near your coughs one of the first images that springs to mind is that they have COVID-19, and you are now infected. Is this a reasonable intrusive thought?

There are numerous reasons for someone to cough, you may also be wearing a mask and have your vaccinations.

Taking a practical approach helps you to determine whether the trigger warrants the thought.

For those thoughts that blindside you and don't seem to come from a logical occurrence, consider whether they go against your values.

An image of you hurting another human might be strongly against your beliefs, which is why it upsets you so much. For a sociopathic serial killer, the image isn't going to have the same impact. When you can clearly define your core values, you will understand why these thoughts cause such a strong reaction.

2. Let these thoughts pass through you

We can't block them or avoid them. Pretending they don't exist may cause you mind to give the thoughts more attention and this will be harder for you to overcome. To minimize the effect of the intrusive thought, accept it, acknowledge it, and visualize the thought passing through you as you move on.

3. Try not to react to fear or with fear

Although difficult, it's essential that you remember that this is only a thought and what you think or imagine is not a reality. If you imagine yourself as poor and homeless, it doesn't mean that you are or you are destined to be. We can feel an immense amount of fear from our intrusive thoughts, but we can't let the fear control us so that we end up doing something that isn't sensible.

Recognize that just because this thought has appeared doesn't mean that you have to act on it. Take a moment for some slow, deep breaths and with every breath, exhale that fear while the tension is released from your body.

4. Don't take your intrusive thoughts to heart

These are not messages from your subconscious describing your underlying desires. They are thoughts that you cannot control and do not make you a bad person. Feeling bad or even guilty about something that isn't reality and hasn't happened is only going to add to the mental strain.

Remind yourself how easy it is to let go of positive thoughts. You imagine you are going to win the lottery; you tell yourself it's not going to happen and move on without further emotions. Practice this with intrusive thoughts.

5. Don't change your life based on your thoughts

I have seen people avoid airports because of frightening images, parties because they fear they will make a fool of themselves, even driving a car because of thoughts of hitting a pedestrian.

People that change the way they live based on their intrusive thoughts aren't going to stop the thoughts. It just leads to living a life based on fears, which is heartbreaking as you can miss out on so much. Deal with the intrusive thoughts head on rather than trying to adjust your reality.

How to Stop Taking Other's Opinions to Heart

The worst advice I have heard time and time again is "Don't take things so personally." That's a wonderful idea but where is the advice? How do I actually do this? Wouldn't it be great just to have a thicker layer of skin and let others' opinions bounce straight off you? For most of us, it isn't that easy and it's a huge cause for rumination.

Here is how other people's opinions cause us to overthink. If you hold the door open for someone and they don't thank you, it is disrespectful. Our mind leads us to think that we are not worthy of respect, which can ruminate into feelings of worthlessness. If people look at you as if you have no worth, perhaps this is true.

Albert Ellis, the father of Rational Emotive Behavior Therapy, would tell you that it isn't the action that causes your emotions, but how you interpret the action. This interpretation is based on our beliefs.

If your belief is that it is polite to hold a door open for others, then you will be upset when you aren't thanked. If you don't believe it is necessary to hold the door open for people, or recognize that not everyone shares your belief, the action won't trigger the same emotions. The same theory can be applied to pretty much all of our actions. Consider the following acts and how your beliefs may differ from someone else's:

• Sharing food, office supplies, information

• Returning missed calls

• Tidying up after yourself

• Family occasions

• Changing the radio station in someone else's car

• Drinking the last of the milk and not replacing it or apologizing

Your partner might find it a huge nag that you always want them to go to family meals. You may feel that they don't like your family or don't want to spend time with you.

From their point of view, they grew up in a broken home and family occasions cause them to think about a childhood they missed out on. Not everyone will share your belief and by understanding this, it becomes easier not to take their actions personally.

Remember that not everything a person says is directly aimed at you. A pet peeve of mine is people who have large cars but are unable to park them. If I happened to mention this to you and you have a big car, it doesn't mean I am criticizing your parking. It's easy to take general comments and turn them into a personal criticism.

Instead of taking these general comments to heart and then ruminating about it for the rest of the day, you can politely ask the person if the comment was aimed at you. Yes, this will mean overcoming a fear of being criticized, but what's the worst that can happen?

If the comment was aimed at you, you can decide whether it is justified or not. If it is justified, you can make an improvement. If not, you can remind yourself that their opinion isn't based on facts but solely their opinion. It's just as likely that they say it wasn't about you, and the rumination is stopped in an instant.

Empathy is a great help here. We are stuck in our own minds and trying to overcome our own problems. People may snap at us, gossip about us, or even just flat out lie. You have to get good at being the bigger person and to do this, don't drink in their poisonous opinions but instead, understand that they might be struggling with their own demons.

They too probably have negative thoughts and fears, problems they are trying to get to the bottom of. It's not fair or right that they take it out on you, but their opinions may be a manifestation of their own problems. How you react may only fuel them into hurting you more.

Make Wise Decisions and Solve Problems Faster

A common complaint is that our rumination creates a fuzzy blur in our mind; there is no clarity to our thinking, and this has a detrimental effect on our decision-making abilities. It's tempting to envy those who are good at solving problems. They seem confident in their abilities and life appears to be more straightforward without all of the doubts.

Decision making is a learned skill. Some are naturally better at it than others but that's not to say that you can't improve your abilities. It's not that you can't make a decision, the problem is that your over-thinking clouds your judgment and causes you to doubt yourself.

Don't tell yourself not to overthink a decision. Instead, we are going to learn how to think smarter so that we can make the right choice with confidence.

Let's say you have to make a decision between a digital presentation and a hard copy of your information. Everyone is going digital, it looks flashier and professional but you feel that a tangible copy of information that clients can take away with them will be more beneficial. Your colleagues convinced you to go with the digital presentation last time and the results weren't as your boss had hoped.

There is a lot riding on this decision, and you feel the pressure mounting up. To make any decision wisely, the first thing to do is remove emotions and focus on facts. If there isn't data supporting an option, then it is an emotion. It's not to say that there isn't room for emotions in decision making, but they will cause you to ruminate.

Take yourself out of the situation and view the problem as an outsider. In this case, you could see things from your boss's point of view or the client's. What would be the most beneficial solution for them? Why are your colleagues so dead set against the idea? Is it because it involves more preparation? If so, how can you overcome this?

Solid decisions are made based on knowledge. Before even weighing the pros and cons of each possible outcome, ask yourself if you have sufficient knowledge. Knowledge can come from a wide range of sources. You might find that research on your clients tells you more about their likes, dislikes, and values.

Being assertive with your colleagues gives you a chance to listen to their thoughts and ideas, opening up new perspectives. Asking your boss for feedback on the last presentation highlights mistakes that were made and areas for improvement.

Finally, take a pen and paper and write down the potential outcomes of each of your options. Look at the worst- and best-case scenarios for each. Once you have weighed the options, which has more pros and cons?

Always set a deadline for decision making. If you really can't see a clear option, play the 1,2,3 game. No prior thinking and no delay in your response. Count 1,2,3 and say the first option that comes to mind. This works better when someone else is counting and you aren't expecting it, and your answer must be said aloud. Though you are lacking in confidence, it doesn't mean your gut instincts are wrong. The 1,2,3 game gives your intuition a chance to shine.

Put It into Practice

I know there are already many ideas that can help you to eliminate rumination but there is one final idea that I find fascinating and the studies prove its effectiveness. Self-distancing, and more specifically, the Batman Effect, are methods we can use to put distance between ourselves and our problems or challenges. This distance enables us to see things from a different perspective.

Self-distancing is the practice of thinking in the second person or using your own name. Rather than saying "I wish I could work harder" you would say "You wish you could work harder" or "*Your name* wishes they could work harder." When we use pronouns other than I, it has a similar effect to giving advice to a friend.

Many successful people, such as Beyoncé and Adele, have alternate personalities that they have created. When they imagine themselves as these people, they are better able to cope with nervousness and stress.

Researchers at the University of Minnesota (2016) asked children aged 4 to 6 to work on a repetitive task for 10 minutes. They had the option to take breaks if they wanted. The children were asked to repeat one of the three following questions as they worked:

- Am I hardworking?

- Is (their name) hardworking?

- Is (their favorite character, i.e., Batman, Dora the Explorer) hardworking?

Those who used their name performed better than those who used the first person. But it was those who imagined themselves as their favorite character that took fewer breaks, worked harder, and enjoyed the activity more. In fact, these children spent 23% more time on the task at hand compared with the children thinking in the third person.

The next time rumination rears its head, try self-distancing or creating your own alternate persona so that you have a little more space to think about the situation in a different, and often more rational, way.

Up to now, we have spent the majority of the time focusing on strategies to beat negative thinking and rumination. You now have a massive range of tips and tricks, backed by science. However, with the constraint strain and pressure we face today, high amounts of stress can quickly undo the work we have done. In the next chapter, we are going to cover some essential tips on how to kick stress to the curb.

CHAPTER 5: REWIRE YOUR BRAIN, RULE YOUR MIND, AND REDUCE STRESS

Without wanting to bombard your mind with statistics, I do feel it is crucial to understand how much stress affects us. Because we all seem to be under stress, it has almost become the norm rather than something that only occurs once in a while. In reality, our bodies aren't designed to cope with constant stress, and we are starting to see how damaging this is.

Some of the statistics below are shocking, but perhaps exactly what we need to realize is that we have to start acting toward a less-stressed lifestyle.

• People between 30 and 49 are the most stressed in the U.S.

• 52% of Generation Z has been diagnosed with mental health issues.

• 83% of U.S. workers suffer from work-related stress

• 1 million people miss work every day because of stress

- Depression costs companies $51 billion in absenteeism

- Healthcare costs from stress cost $190 billion annually

- Work-related stress causes 120,000 deaths in the U.S. each year

(The American Institute of Stress, 2019)

None of us want to be a part of any of the above statistics! So, it's essential that we take control of stress and see it for what it is, fuel for unhappiness, negativity, and health problems and not something that we can afford to just accept.

What the Neuroscientists Tell Us

So, you are stressed out and feel like you are on the verge of exploding. Something has to give, and you don't want to cause a scene or breakdown. We have 4 instant stress busters that you may or may not have heard of.

The problem is, because they are so simple, you might not feel they are powerful enough to work. For this reason, I have included neuroscience research to help convince you.

1. Tense and relax facial muscles

There is a communication loop between your brain and your body. When the gray matter in your brain gets stressed, various muscles tense up. Once your muscles are tense, a message is sent back to the brain to let it know that the message has been received.

If you have tried asking your brain to stop stressing and it hasn't worked, you need to break the loop by making your body tell your brain that you are not stressed anymore. Releasing the facial muscles that were tensed sends that message. As you might imagine, the facial muscles are the best to use because they are more closely linked to our emotions. That being said, your hands, stomach, and more surprisingly, your bum muscles will also send the right messages to the brain (bakadesuyo.com).

2. Rapid breathing

Yes, this will surprise you because we generally focus on the benefits of slow breathing, which can also be used to help reduce stress and feel calmer. But what about when we need to feel more excited, and that adrenaline rush is going to work in our favor? Deep breathing (even used by Navy Seal recruits) activates the parasympathetic nervous system, necessary to conserve energy.

On the contrary, the sympathetic nervous system drives our fight or flight response. Normally, we would work on controlling the fight or flight response. But don't forget that there are some situations where it works in our favor. Maybe you need that rush of energy to tick off that to-do list or get excited about a challenge.

3. Jolt your vagus nerve

The vagus nerve is the longest nerve in the body. It extends from the brain to the large intestine and is responsible for a number of key body functions. For us in particular, lowering the heart rate and managing stress and anxiety. If this nerve is damaged, you may suffer from a lower attention span and even depression (Dr. Shelly Sethi, n.d.).

The vagus nerve passes around the throat muscles and is attached to the vocal cords. Singing or chanting can jolt your vagus nerve. Alternatively, you can splash your face with cold water—a classic example of a traditional technique that you may have previously dismissed.

4. Love your music

If you put on your all-time classic tunes, you will be tempted to sing, waking up the vagus nerve. But music can also help stress levels in other ways. Music engages a large part of the limbic system that is responsible for our emotional responses. Music also increases the heart rate and, science aside, you know those songs that just make you feel better no matter what mood you are in.

Making music has a stronger effect on the limbic system. Nevertheless, not all of us share this talent. Remember that music is the key; if you don't play an instrument, dancing also brings about other benefits such as exercise releasing endorphins and, if you want to dance it out with your friends, the positive impact of social interactions.

From personal experience and the feedback from clients, these 4 brain tricks are extremely effective. Naturally, if you are in the middle of a meeting, you probably don't want to start making strange faces or bursting out with your favorite tune but squeezing your bum muscles is a subtle alternative.

If you start to feel stress building up before an important event or even while sitting at your desk, popping to the bathroom and splashing your face with cold water could alter your mindset and the following outcomes. None of the solutions take more than a couple of minutes.

How to Declutter Your Mind

"Clutter is nothing more than postponed decisions."

— *BARBARA HEMPHILL*

What is clutter in the mind? It's not necessarily a case of negative thoughts. It is everything in our brains that really serves little to no purpose. Often, this clutter is full of past memories, mistakes we have made and are holding on to, or even those things that are out of our control. It's the things we need to do and worries about the future.

Basically, it's everything that stops us from concentrating on the task at hand and the present. This excessive buzzing in our minds can greatly affect our mood, increase anxiety levels, and lead to depression. Much like negative thoughts, clutter is very hard to switch off.

Understand that there is a link between physical clutter and mental clutter. Researchers spent three days touring the homes of dual-income couples. The women who used vocabulary like clutter and unfinished had higher levels of depression throughout the day. Women who used more positive words like restful and restored were happier overall (Saxbe & Repetti, 2009).

In Chapter 3, we looked at how to declutter your home. So, if you haven't started, now is a good time.

Writing is an extremely powerful tool for decluttering the mind. Writing to-do lists before going to sleep encourages a restful night without worrying about what needs to be done. Brain dumping is a quick technique that can be used to declutter in a particular moment. Of course, daily journaling will allow you to remove some of the clutter each day so that it doesn't overwhelm you.

How you handle your decisions will affect the amount of clutter your brain stores. As Barbara Hemphill said, each postponed decision is going to add to the clutter. Some of our decisions should be put on auto-pilot. It sounds a little boring but how often do you ruminate over what to have for dinner?

When you have a plan for the week, there is no need to think about it every day. The same can be said for your clothes, household tasks, exercise routines, and so on. Routine is our best friend because it reduces a lot of the simple decisions.

For more difficult decisions, don't delay them. The sooner you tackle each one, the less clutter you have on your mind.

• Write down the problem and the best outcome.

• Brainstorm at least three solutions that will get you to the outcome.

• Come up with a list of pros and cons for each.

• Play out each solution in your mind, look for the tools or resources you will need and the possible setbacks for each.

• Eliminate the worst solution.

- Review the pros and cons of the remaining solutions based on how each one played out.

- If there is still no clear option, remember the 1,2,3 game!

When we declutter our homes, we are going to start with one area and work our way bit by bit. It doesn't make sense to split up our energy and attempt to multi-task.

Take the same approach with your mind. Visualize the clutter in your mind, push it all to one side and focus only on one thing. Any time the rest of that clutter starts to push its way into your free space, strengthen the barrier so that the one task remains alone.

Another tip is to not let so much clutter into your mind in the first place. There are a variety of clutter sources that we need to limit our exposure to or just cut out completely. Pay attention to how you feel after scrolling through social media or watching the news. Do you feel happier? Is it adding to your quality of life? Is it necessary? If the answer is no, you are letting in clutter.

Once you have dumped all that is not necessary and limited the information coming in, it's time to prioritize the clutter that is left. This may require one final brain dump which can then be organized into a list beginning with the most important. You may also want to create time for a weekly or even daily brain dump and prioritize the remaining clutter.

Rewire Your Brain to Overcome Stressful Thought Patterns

We briefly talked about neuroplasticity, but in order to rewire your brain, you have to first understand exactly how it works. There is a common expression among neurologists: "neurons that fire together wire together." This means that each time we fire up a thought, the neurons stick together creating new connections and memories based on our experiences.

Think of it like Play-Doh. Have you or your child ever stuck two colors together and then regretted it because you know they won't separate? Every time we stress about something, more Play-Doh is getting stuck together.

Scientists used to believe that after puberty the brain was fully formed and wouldn't change. The Play-Doh is destined to remain the same. Thanks to technologies such as MRI scans, we have now discovered that we can develop our brains and rewire them. The Play-Doh doesn't have to be doomed!

The pandemic has caused so much stress for probably the majority of the world, but there has been some good to come out of it. During lockdowns, many people turned to learning new hobbies at home. The more people practiced these hobbies, the stronger the new connections in the brain become, creating neural networks.

Rewiring the brain to overcome stress sounds more complicated than it actually is. One of the simplest ways you can start today is by taking up a new hobby. You will gain more benefits if the hobby is active but don't discount others.

In 2015, research published in NeuroImage showed that visual art like painting and drawing alters neural structure and function. Learning a new musical instrument is also excellent for neuroplasticity because it requires complex cognitive processes that reorganize neural networks.

Here are some further thoughts on what you can do to help develop your brain so that stressful thought patterns are reduced and controlled:

1. Mentally practice activities

In some cases, it is not always possible to go about the activity we would like to. A person who has had a stroke might not be able to walk, but by mentally imagining the process, the neurons are still being activated.

2. Learn a new language

Learning languages boosts both gray and white brain matter. Gray matter is associated with your attention, memory, and emotions.

White matter helps different areas of your brain to communicate and can help you with problem-solving. Studies show that learning a new language increases the density of gray brain matter (Lindgren et al.,2012).

3. Keep up with puzzles

Crosswords, word searches, and sudokus keep the mind active. You are constantly learning and firing up your neurons.

A study involving 19,100 people showed that those who did puzzles had better brain function, even to the equivalent brain function of someone 10 years younger (Brooker et al., 2019).

4. Stress hurts neuroplasticity

Understand that high levels of stress over a long period of time can overpower neuroplasticity—the brain is approximately 2% of our body weight but requires around 20% of our energy.

Chronic stress uses energy that could be used to create new neurons. When stressful thought patterns occur, tell yourself that you are restricting your brain's ability to grow.

Deepak Chopra, an advocate for alternative medicine, executive director of Sharp HealthCare's Center for Mind-Body Medicine, and co-founder of the Chopra Center for Wellbeing, has one 5-minute daily practice for reducing stress and gaining success.

He explains that neuroplasticity combines neurogenesis (the growth of new neurons) and synaptogenesis (the new connections between neurons).

Contemplative meditation, self-reflection, and asking meaningful questions can enhance neuroplasticity.

These types of questions include:

• Who am I?

• What do I want?

• What is my purpose?

• What is my unique talent?

• What is my passion?

• How am I authentic?

- What are my responsibilities?

By taking 5 minutes a day to self-reflect and consider the answers to questions like these, you can create new neurons and new connections. Chopra also says that it must be practiced every day for 6 weeks so that it becomes a lifelong habit.

Be the Master of Your Thoughts

As much as we would like to think that we are the master of our thoughts, there are some additional characters who are excellent at taking control.

There is the inner critic: the character who compares you to others, listens to others' opinions, and believes in your self-doubt and self-blame.

The worrier is obsessed with what-ifs and is often irrational. The reactor is a dangerous one as this character has no impulse control and triggers negative emotions such as anger and annoyance.

Finally, the sleep depriver is a complete ruminator!

In order to become the master of your thoughts, you need to first acknowledge that these characters exist. You need to rise above them and keep them all in place.

Of the four characters, the inner critic is the one who dominates. Get this one under control and the other three fall into place. For this, we will cover the inner critic in more detail in the next section.

Let's take a look at how to gain control of the other three.

1. Controlling the worrier

If the worrier is on high alert for extended periods of time, your health is at risk. The fight or flight response is overworked, and you may experience breathlessness, increased heart rate, and tension in your muscles.

There are two ways to calm the worrier. You can address a higher power, if you believe in it, or address the worrier itself.

Remember that a higher power doesn't necessarily mean God. For some, it might be Buddha, a spirit, or an energy.

For others, it is science, nature, or a completely different eternity you wish to create and name.

If you are worried about your parents becoming ill, thank you higher power for taking care of them, for keeping them safe and healthy.

Alternatively, address your worrier:

Dear Worrier,

Thank you for being so concerned about my parents but it is no longer necessary. I will take care of this issue now. I will call in on them, make sure they are well and doing everything to keep themselves safe. It is no longer your responsibility.

These techniques sound slightly out there but they do work. You are separating yourself from the worry and telling the brain that everything is taken care of.

While addressing something or someone, your mind is not occupied with the worry.

2. Dominating the reactor

The worrier and the reactor present in similar ways, so shortness of breath, increased heart rate, and tension.

It's necessary to first determine which character is taking over the mind.

Is it a dull, constant worry that feels more like an ache, or is it sharp, heated, and forceful?

If it is the reactor, it is essential that you stop this character immediately. There isn't time to run to the bathroom and splash water on your face. By definition, this character will react.

Every time we feel the reactor take control, we have a split second to decide whether this character will win or not. And you may not feel like it, but you are in control of this.

Let's say your boss is publicly humiliating you and you are about to explode. In that split second, you can get angry, or you can try the Buteyko breathing method.

Naturally, inhale and exhale. Once you have exhaled, hold your breath for as long as possible. Hold your nose if it helps. When you need to breathe, let go of your nose and breathe naturally.

This breathing method helps to rebalance the oxygen and carbon dioxide in your body, particularly if you have been breathing too quickly.

3. Governing the sleep depriver

Because the sleep depriver is such a ruminator, you can revise Chapter 4, "Techniques to Stop Rumination and Sleep Better," where we looked at how a routine before bed can help you to relax. The sleep depriver is also provoked by other types of thoughts.

Planning is awesome. It shows that we are looking forward to things in the future and that we are trying to manage our time the most effectively. Nevertheless, for some people, this planning becomes compulsive and the inner planner in us leads to sleep deprivation. This comes about when it becomes necessary to plan every minute of the day. When things don't go to plan, we feel overwhelming amounts of stress.

In order not to let the inner planner take over your sleep, try to create a weekly routine and stick to it as much as possible.

As part of this routine, be sure to include some buffer times. If it takes 10 minutes to get from the school drop off to work, add a 5-minute buffer in case of traffic. This will relieve the pressure of not sticking to the plan if something unexpected comes up.

You should also try to save some free time on the weekends too. This downtime can be used in case you didn't get to complete everything in your plan or for just relaxing.

Strategies to Outsmart Your Inner Critic

Our inner critics are experts at negative self-talk. They are the names and insults we call ourselves; it's when we tell ourselves off for the things we do or even the thoughts we have. Our inner critics must be stopped immediately because they can quickly spiral out of control.

For this reason, we need quick solutions to interrupt the particular critical thought you are experiencing. We can do this by using some of the techniques we have looked at, flicking a rubber band on your wrist, changing your environment, or changing your activity.

Visualization and creating a persona for your inner critic will also help. If you can imagine your inner critic as a character, you can address it. Tell the character to "Pack it in" or "That's enough now." Whatever the negative self-talk is, replace it with a positive. Your inner critic would say "You were such an idiot." Your replacement sentence should be "You made a mistake, and you are going to learn from this."

You can't just believe what your inner critic is telling you. It's not easy to do this because you still need to improve your self-esteem. With greater self-esteem, the words of the inner critic can be dismissed because you feel more confident about yourself, your abilities, and the decisions you make.

Still, until this moment, analyze what this character is telling you and decide if your character has the evidence to back this up. If there is no evidence, there is no basis for their words.

Finally, consider what would happen if your inner critic was right. What would be the outcome if you took this persona and said, "So what?" or "And?" Your inner critic is telling you that you totally embarrassed yourself with that political statement you made. And? Are all of your friends going to abandon you because you voiced your opinion, or will they just move on?

You made a bad joke at work. People didn't laugh, but you certainly aren't going to lose your job over it. When we challenge the inner voice in this way, you will find that it quickly shuts up as there is no response.

Don't forget that you can use your inner critic to your advantage. Sometimes, and only sometimes, you can accept what this voice is telling you. Maybe you don't have the skill to achieve a certain task. We have already learned that this can be changed. Don't ruminate on what you can do but decide how you can improve yourself.

Just a quick reminder that, of the four characters that try to control our thoughts, the inner critic is the puppet master. Negative self-talk will cause you to worry, lose sleep, and to react with anger or frustration. The inner critic in us destroys any self-esteem we have left. And if you do start to build some up, if the inner critic still has control, it will just tear you down again.

Stress Management in 10 Steps

Stress management is more than just managing your stress levels. It's about recognizing what triggers your stress and using techniques to reduce the effects. It's also about accepting the fact that we will never be completely free from stress. Firstly, because there is too much going on in the world and our lives for this to happen. Secondly, a small amount of stress can be good for us.

There have been numerous studies on the negative effects of stress. However, in 2016, Daniela Kaufer, Elizabeth Kirby, and their colleagues at the University of California, Berkeley, discovered that the right type and amount of stress can help us.

Their studies on rats showed that acute, short-lived stress doubled the creation of new neurons in the hippocampus. These are the same neurons that are generated when we learn new skills (think back to our neuroplasticity). The rats also performed better on a memory test. So, the right amount of stress for a short period of time can improve the brain and keep us more alert.

This is why we need to manage our stress levels to a point where it can serve some good. Imagine you are preparing for a party. No stress and you won't have the sense of urgency to get things done. Too much stress and you become overwhelmed to the point that you rush around but aren't actually doing anything. The right amount gives you the rush of adrenaline to achieve the things on your list.

Before implementing any of the stress-management techniques, spend some time thinking about what your stress triggers are. Don't be surprised if you have a list and things get added to them over a day or two. Sometimes, we don't always remember stress triggers until they actually occur.

Realistically, there are potentially hundreds, even thousands, of stress triggers depending on the type of person. The most common are family, work, finances, and change. That being said, things like traffic, COVID-19, a messy home, and so many other things could be enough to start feeling the tension.

Once you have your list of stressors, you can start to recognize the stress signals for each one. Do you feel yourself panicking or sweating; do you get headaches or stomach aches, feel dizzy, etc. By knowing the stress signals, you can start to implement stress-management strategies.

- **Reduce background noise:** Whether it's the TV or you are in a crowded place, try to reduce the noise that is around you. The continuous stimuli can make your stress worse.

- **Talk about the cause of your stress:** If someone does something that irritates you, politely let them know. Coming home to a load of dishes when you left the home clean is annoying. Having people take things from your desk and not return them stops you from getting your work done.

- **Self-massage:** Start with your left hand, take your right thumb and index finger and place them on the top and bottom of the base of your left thumb. Rub your thumb from the base to the tip and repeat the same for each finger and then the right hand.

- **Find a park:** As little as 10 minutes in a natural setting can reduce the effects of mental and physical stress and make you feel happier (Cornell University, 2020).

- **Help others:** Research from Yale University School of Medicine (2015) found that helping others can improve our overall mood. This could be a friend, a coworker, or even just holding the door open for someone.

- **Take a power nap:** A short nap between 10 to 20 minutes can reduce stress hormone levels such as cortisol.

- **Hugs and kisses:** Hugging someone and/or kissing them can lower cortisol levels—particularly for women. If you are lucky enough to still get that heart flutter, kissing can also give you a burst of adrenaline. You also get a rush of happy hormones like dopamine and serotonin.

- **Chew gum:** The studies are still producing mixed results on the effects of chewing gum and stress. However, the U.S. Army has included chewing gum in combat rations as a way for soldiers to manage stress since World War I.

- **Smell the roses:** Maybe not the roses, but aromatherapy is highly effective for stress management. Certain smells can alter activity in the brain waves and lower stress hormones. Experiment with different scents—one man's pleasure is another man's pain!

- **Be grateful:** Start the day thinking about 3 things you are grateful for, keep a magnetic whiteboard on your fridge and leave gratitude messages or keep a gratitude journal. People who are more grateful have better mental health and less stress (Valikhani et al., 2018).

You are probably wondering why I haven't mentioned the most obvious stress management techniques like meditation, exercise, and a healthy diet. All of these things are crucial, but I prefer to look at these types of activities as self-care that leads to a less stressful lifestyle. In Chapter 7, we will be going over strategies to take care of ourselves.

Put It into Practice

While having a multitude of options to rewire your brain and reduce stress, if you struggle to make decisions, more options aren't going to help you. Also, the more options you have, the easier it becomes to give up on one and switch to another.

For this reason, to put this chapter into practice, we are going to create a personalized tool kit with one technique from each section. This is how I started my practice:

➔ What the neuroscientists say: I loved the idea of splashing water on my face. Understanding how this works made me believe more in the effects.

➔ Rewire the brain: I am a bit of a sudoku fan but never make the time. Each morning with my coffee, I did a quick puzzle.

➔ Mastering my thoughts: I felt that of the characters, the worrier was my most dominant. So, I created a persona and learned to distance myself from it.

➔ My inner critic: I wanted a more assertive approach, so I chose "So what."

➔ Stress management: I liked the idea of nature and chewing gum.

Once you have chosen one from each section, stick to them for at least a few weeks and keep a note of any changes you experience. If, after a few weeks, you aren't feeling the benefits, go for another option.

It's all well and good learning to overcome negative thinking, rumination, and manage your stress. But what happens if it is other people who are the continuous source of your mental health issues. In the next chapter, we will take a look at some of the behaviors of others that add to our difficulties and what to do when negative thinking becomes more serious.

CHAPTER 6: THROW AWAY NEGATIVITY, TOXICITY, AND PASSIVE AGGRESSION LIKE WORN-OUT SHOES

L et's say that you have been working extra hard on some of the techniques and you are starting to see some improvements. All of a sudden, a factor from the outside world comes along and screws things up. It's not just that we have gone back to square one, it feels like things are worse.

Any setback with the progress we make is going to affect our confidence and cause us to doubt our abilities to move forward. Never forget that just because you have had a setback, it doesn't mean that your strategies aren't working. You don't have to start from scratch. You do need to control the negative thoughts so they don't spiral and cause you to remain stuck in this setback. Immediate action is necessary.

These setbacks are often because of external factors. Perhaps a relationship ends or you lose a loved one. Or there is that one person or situation in your life that is blocking your progress toward positivity.

So, what do you do when your home is far safer than braving it out into the world? Or when Marcus from accounting just won't stop taking digs at you?

We leave this chapter toward the end because these are the more challenging obstacles we need to face when overcoming negativity. This is because it's not just about dealing with your demons, it's about overcoming things that are even more out of your control.

With what you have learned so far, you will be feeling more in control of your emotions and thought patterns. These are our fundamentals because, to cope with external factors, you have to feel stronger, both with your negative thinking and other conditions like anxiety and depression.

Let's look at Marcus from accounting as an example. Before Chapter 1, Marcus would constantly make jokes about your abilities, intelligence, or even your appearance. You would have listened, taken it to heart, and ruminated on his words.

Now, you know that you first have to reflect on Marcus' words and determine if there is any truth to them. You have practiced the techniques, so the negative thinking doesn't spiral and you are handling this stress. But Marcus doesn't stop!

Now that you are in a better mental place, it's time to work on Marcus. You can't control what other people do but you can control how you react.

How to Triumph Over Social Anxiety

In the U.S. alone, there are approximately 15 million people suffering from social anxiety (Anxiety & Depression

Association of America, 2020). At first, you might think that social anxiety is just an extreme case of shyness.

People who are shy will come across as quiet, they may easily blush, and it seems they aren't interested in making new friends. Social anxiety is a phobia of any type of social interaction. It's not that they don't want to make friends— it's that they can't.

A big part of social anxiety will be not wanting to go out to public places for fear of making a fool of themselves or being judged.

It can get to the point where people can't relax, eat, or speak naturally in front of others. It can affect relationships, prevent promotions at work, and stop you from living a fulfilling life.

There is absolutely no doubt that social anxiety has increased significantly since the pandemic. The actual number of people could be far higher than 15 million considering those who haven't been diagnosed.

The fear of any contact with people has caused even those without social anxiety to rethink whether they interact with others. For those who already were terrified of society, it has only confirmed the fear.

When it comes to illnesses, coronavirus or others, you need to look at your personal circumstances and the mental model of probability. For people who are vaccinated, the chances of becoming seriously ill are greatly reduced. If you wear a mask, catching COVID-19 is greatly reduced. Combined with social distancing, the risk is very low.

When a phobia kicks in, our irrational brain will often overpower any science or logic we try to feed it. Ask yourself about the causes of your social anxiety because nothing is black or white.

Two people can have social anxiety. One is terrified of catching a fatal virus, the next could feel suffocated in a group of people, pandemic or not. A third might not be worried about getting sick but freeze at the thought of an interview.

The fourth knows there is something wrong but can't understand why the following symptoms are appearing:

• Increased heart rate, breathlessness, sweating

• Shaking

• The mind going blank

• Avoiding questions

• Lightheadedness/dizziness

• A feeling of sickness or vomiting

• A heightened self-consciousness

• Missing school or work

• Excessive worrying before an event

• Relying on alcohol or drugs to face a social situation

Anytime you start to notice these symptoms arising when you are in social situations, make a note of your surroundings and the likely triggers.

Make two lists: one for things that make you extremely uncomfortable and another for the social situations that are impossible.

As we have seen before, it is essential that we question these fears. With the list of situations that make you anxious, write down the realistic worst-case scenario. When we say realistic, it's because our fears could blow the worst-case scenario out of proportion.

Your fear might be about running a meeting and your worst-case scenario could be your manager criticizing you in front of your clients. This isn't going to happen because that is unprofessional of the manager. A realistic worst-case scenario is that you make a mistake.

Thinking about the worst-case scenario may seem like it's thinking in the negative. But we have to appreciate that actively thinking about the worst-case scenario of our fears allows us to prepare for a solution. It's not the same as ruminating on what may happen.

Another thing to check is your social skills. Don't take this the wrong way, but sometimes, our fears are based on past experiences where we have misread a situation.

You may have detected disdain but really it was a poor attempt at sarcasm. Quite often we think people are staring at us when they might just be daydreaming.

If people are the main concern for your social anxiety, it is worth learning more about tone of voice, body language, and facial expressions so that you get better at correctly reading people.

Put It into Practice

Overcoming social anxiety is a very gradual process. and we take small steps to remain in control. If you have spent two months locked in your apartment because of quarantine, you aren't going to aim straight for a movie theater or concert.

The goal is to walk to the end of the street. The next day, go to the end of the street and sit on a bench. If you are terrified of going back to the office, the first step is to make it to your desk. For now, avoid places like the break room or kitchen where there is likely to be groups of people. You can build up to this when you are comfortable at your desk.

Create a goal for overcoming your anxiety. Break the goal down into small, manageable steps. Don't forget that with each step you succeed, you need to have a reward to keep you motivated toward the bigger picture.

Top Tips for Depression

Depression looks different for each person. One of my clients described it as feeling like you have lost something but have no idea what it is or where it might be. After a while, you realize that you have lost yourself. It's the same feeling you get when you look in the mirror and don't recognize the reflection.

Some have described it as the sensation of drowning or suffocating but everyone around you seems to be breathing normally and can't see your struggles. For others, it's complete numbness. It's not about being sad or crying all the time. You just don't feel anything.

Most people will agree that depression is exhausting. But what is more exhausting is pretending to the rest of the world that everything is OK. You are tired and you are scared, but you are too tired for the flight response and too scared for the fight response.

For an accurate diagnosis, you need to consult your doctor as they might prescribe medication and/or refer you to a therapist. There are various online questionnaires that will give you an idea of the degree of your depression. I like psycom.net because there is no need to give any personal information, create an account, or enter your email address.

Depression doesn't just go away. Regardless of whether your depression is moderate or severe, you must take action. Don't forget that the next chapter looks at self-care, which will also help with depression. Here are some other ideas that can relieve the symptoms of depression.

1. Don't suppress your feelings

We often feel that expressing our emotions today is wrong. That social acceptance is all about keeping ourselves pulled together. This is the absolute opposite of what you need to do. Studies show that bottling up feelings increased the chances of premature death from all causes by over 30%. The risk of being diagnosed with cancer increased by 70% (Chapman et al., 2013).

Give yourself time to hurt, or cry, or shout. But it has to be a dedicated period of time so that you don't get stuck in this state. Most definitely set a timer and tell yourself that when the timer goes off, it's time to get active. This can be an amazing sense of relief and you can feel the weight of pressure lifting.

2. Remind yourself that today is not a predictor of tomorrow

This works both ways. Just because today is a good day and you are feeling more positive, it's not a sign that your depression has gone.

I know this sounds negative, but without intervention, you will continue with the rollercoaster of ups and downs. So a good day is not a sign to stop working on your symptoms.

On the other hand, you also have to remind yourself that even if today was a shockingly bad day and you couldn't bring yourself off the sofa, tomorrow is not guaranteed to be the same.

3. Fight what the depression is telling you

This might be the hardest, but it will also be the most beneficial. On the days when your depression is telling you that there is no point in staying in bed, you have to fight it.

Don't think about all that you need to do or should do. It's about one small step.

You need to get your feet onto the floor. Get down to the kitchen or get in the shower.

If you don't want to meet your friends, fight this voice with a counterargument that it beats staying home alone. It will go against everything your body is telling you, but your mind has to take control.

4. Expand your horizons

According to the National Health Service in the U.K., learning new skills has various positive effects on mental health aside from creating new brain neurons. Picking up a new hobby can create a sense of purpose while increasing your self-esteem. If you are not yet ready to start an activity where you meet new people, you can volunteer at an animal shelter.

Fixing things is an awesome way to feel a great sense of achievement. There are so many DIY and hack videos online that you can start some projects at home like revamping an old wardrobe. There are also hundreds of free online courses for you to gain new qualifications and learn more about yourself.

5. Limit social media

This goes back to limiting the amount of negative information you take in. It's not just the depressing news that we see. Social media can make us feel angry, even jealous. One study showed that people who checked their Facebook at night were more inclined to feel unhappy and depressed (Lyall et al., 2018).

However, those who spent less time on their social media accounts reported showing fewer symptoms of depression and loneliness (Hunt et al., 2018).

Social media does have its good sides, and it's hard to imagine not having at least one account. Think about limiting the content you can see and blocking those who post a lot of negativity.

Put It into Practice

Many times, depression takes over because we can't see anything to look forward to. Again, we are still sticking to the small-scale things that are easier to achieve. So, don't start thinking about the next big family celebration as you might feel worse. Plan things that you know you will enjoy. A good way to see the gray cloud lifting is to plan:

• 7 small daily activities (10 minutes of exercise, a chapter of your book, listening to music)

• 1 weekly activity (a soak in the tub, takeout, a movie)

• 1 bigger monthly activity (a new piece of clothing, day trip to a different city, haircut)

Be careful about planning things that rely on others, just in case they can't join you. That's not to say that you can't sign up for a regular group activity.

Overcoming Passive Aggression

Passive aggression is when people express their negative feelings in a way that harms others.

There are two ways this can affect us. We could be the passive-aggressive person, or people around us are acting in this way and causing you harm.

First, let's identify some passive-aggressive behaviors:

• Excessive sarcasm or backhanded compliments

• The silent treatment

• Purposely being late

- Playing the victim

- Backing out of commitments at the last minute (knowing it will cause you problems)

- Doing things that they know will annoy others (overfilling the trash instead of emptying it)

- Keeping score

- Reverse psychology

- Shifting responsibility

- Pretending they don't understand something

If passive-aggressive behavior is something you need to work on, you have to understand that you have the right to feel angry or upset. If your partner has hurt you, you might retreat and, without realizing it, give them the silent treatment.

Our passive-aggressive behavior is because something is causing us to suffer but we don't have the right skills or confidence to deal with it correctly. A lot of the time, we are scared of potential confrontation. We end up being too passive, too aggressive, or passive-aggressive. None will resolve the issue. We need to work on our assertive skills.

Put It into Practice:

If your passive aggression is because you find it difficult to deal with other people's behavior, first identify the triggers. What are they doing or what have they said? Next, it goes back to that split second when you have a choice. Don't react! As the brain releases all of these emotion hormones, this isn't the best time to respond.

When you are at home, comfortable, and more relaxed, you need to plan what you want to say and how you are going to say it so that you are assertive yet still polite and kind.

1. Understand exactly why you are having negative emotions. Be precise about your feelings. If you are disappointed, don't say sad. If you are furious, don't say angry.

2. Prepare what you want to say to the person and practice this, either in the mirror or with someone you trust.

3. Use "I" statements. This is an invaluable tip. "I" statements keep the focus on your feelings rather than beginning with "You," which comes across as blaming the other person.

4. Keep check of your body language. Assertion requires the right amount of eye contact and an open posture without having your hands behind your back or clenched together in your lap.

5. Keep check of your voice. The tone of voice is one thing but so is the speed. Too fast and you seem nervous, too slow and you might seem like you are talking to them as if they are stupid.

6. Suggest a solution or a consequence if the behavior continues. For example, "No, I can't work overtime tonight but I can tomorrow," or "If you keep disrespecting me in front of my friends, I won't invite you again."

7. Apologize if necessary. Nobody is perfect and, if you have made a mistake with past behaviors, it's OK to admit this.

When others are passive-aggressive toward you, you can't let it slide. This will add to everything we have worked at overcoming in the previous chapters. Just as being assertive can help you overcome your own passive-aggressive behavior; it will help you with others too. This is because you are addressing the problem directly.

Make an extra effort to control your emotions with passive-aggressive people. Passive-aggressive behavior is closely linked to manipulation. If a person can see that they have got to you, this will fuel them to continue. Think about the facts and the evidence that you have. This is why it is better to choose a time to be assertive rather than react in the moment—at least for now.

It's not your job to change the passive-aggressive people in your life. You have enough on your plate dealing with your own mental health. Plus, as you know, if someone doesn't recognize their behavior or is unwilling to change, they won't. Consider putting some space between yourself and these people. You don't have to eliminate them from your life. But you can limit how much time you spend with them while you are committed to your mental health.

Understand What Toxic Positivity Is and How to Avoid It

Positivity is a good thing. After all, we are striving toward it. So, how can positivity be toxic? Dr. Jamie Zuckerman, a specialist in adult anxiety and depression, explains toxic positivity as the assumption that you should have a positive mindset despite the pain you are feeling.

It's the idea that you can simply change your entire perspective by thinking positive thoughts and feeling those positive vibes. You know what I mean with the hundreds of memes we see. It's the loved ones who try to help with things like "Look on the bright side" and "It could be worse."

All of these statements are true. But they underestimate the extent of the problem. It's as if we can go to bed thinking about the good in our lives and wake up a new person.

What's worse, is that it reinforces the incorrect idea that negative emotions are bad and that we shouldn't have these types of feelings. Positive emotions are pushed onto us, obliging us to put a smile on our faces. Not only are our negative emotions squashed but we also feel bad about ourselves for having them.

The pandemic has seriously increased the amount of toxic positivity everywhere we look. With the millions of people who have lost their lives, the thing we tell ourselves time and time again is that it could be worse.

Yes, it is true that things could be worse. But that doesn't mean to say that you can't feel scared, lonely, confused, and angry. Trying not to think about these thoughts or replacing them with positive ones won't help. On the contrary, it can make the situation worse.

Two groups were asked to verbalize their stream of thoughts for 5 minutes. One group was told not to think of a white bear. The other group was told to think of a white bear. Each time a participant thought about the bear, they rang a bell. The group that was told not to think about the bear rang the bell twice as many times as the other group (Wegner, 1987).

Toxic positivity requires a close examination of your feelings. Journaling is an excellent way to accept your emotions, admitting that they exist. While trying to ignore negative emotions makes them stronger, writing them down reduces how intensely we feel these emotions (UCLA, n.d.).

Very often, we get caught in a mindset of emotions being either positive or negative, or that we have to choose between one or the other. This is still a strategy for not accepting our real emotions. If you are happy, you can't feel guilty about this. If you are angry, you don't need to be ashamed. You can experience positive and negative emotions at the same time.

Take care with toxic positivity in your relationships. If you are having a difficult time, you need your partner not to say things like "Get over it" or "It's not that big a deal." They might not realize what they are doing and assume that they are saying the right things to make you feel better.

Be assertive and use specific adjectives to describe how you feel when others push their toxic positivity on you. Remind them that you don't necessarily need saving or advice. You just need someone to listen and respect your emotions.

Recognize toxic positive thoughts for what they are: any message that excludes the option to validate your real feelings. Encourage others to do the same. When people are talking about how they feel, don't dismiss their true feelings and don't push the toxic positivity on them.

Put It into Practice

So, we have one last exercise that will tie up all of this chapter and literally, throw away the negativity that frequently comes from others.

Take a piece of paper. Write down the negative experience, the emotion, the person, anything that is affecting you. It's not necessarily a brain dump because it is normally just a couple of specific sentences rather than everything on your mind.

Take that piece, rip it up into pieces, and throw them in the trash. It doesn't sound like a lot, but studies have shown that the process of literally throwing them away makes a difference. Once participants in the study had thrown their thoughts away, they no longer thought about them. The participants who carried this paper around with them felt that their thoughts were magnified (Association for Psychological Science, 2012).

The great thing about this is that, as you are writing about the source of your negativity you are processing it. So, you aren't avoiding or suppressing your emotions.

The final chapter is one of awesome optimism and positivity. We are going to end on a high and find out what it takes to find and develop our self-esteem, to make positive thoughts and self-talk a natural habit, and how to start enjoying the present.

CHAPTER 7: YIELD POSITIVE CHANGES AND SEE THE DIFFERENCES IN ALL AREAS OF YOUR LIFE

A s I have mentioned, making a mental change from the negative to the positive isn't a case of waking up and telling yourself to be positive. It takes time, practice, and patience.

Before you begin to start seeing things in a more optimistic light, you need to put the work in to understand and overcome the negative.

Nevertheless, once you are starting to feel that your thought patterns are more neutral, it's a great time to work on encouraging positivity in the different areas of your life.

Please, I can't stress this enough, don't just skip to this chapter without going through the process of relieving your negativity, rumination, anxiety, and depression. You run the risk of the placebo effect. You will feel better for a short period, but the negativity will resurface.

If you feel that negativity is still controlling your life, take some more time to see the effects of the techniques we have been over. It's OK to take this time to get it right. It's a change that will last a lifetime, be patient with yourself. If you are excited about becoming more positive, let's get started.

Positive Thoughts Yield Positive Results

Before the 1980s, positive thinking was a concept with no scientific backing. In 1985, two professors of psychology, Michael F. Scheier and Charles S. Carver, published a study that backed the idea that positive thinking leads to positive results.

They created the Life Orientation Test or LOT, revised in 1989 to LOT-R. It was a way of assessing people's level of optimism. It was first used on a group of university students to understand if there was a link between levels of optimism and health. The results showed that students who were more optimistic had fewer physical symptoms.

Since then, positive thinking has drawn a lot more interest from researchers. This has led to the term dispositional optimism, which is what we are working toward. Dispositional optimism is the belief that our future will have more positive events and experiences than negative ones. This type of optimism encourages a great range of well-being benefits, specifically reduced depression, anxiety, and stress.

Being more optimistic and thinking positively doesn't block the stress or worries. It does, however, help you to find the solutions to problems by looking at outcomes in a more favorable way.

So, how does positive thinking lead to positive results? Those with a more positive outlook on life are more determined to achieve their goals. With lower stress levels, they are better at coping with pressure. Setbacks aren't something that stop positive thinkers from achieving their goals. Instead, they will use them as learning experiences.

Here are some ways you can start introducing a little bit of positivity into each day and get more results.

1. Smile

Even if you don't feel happy, smile. When you smile, your brain has a little positivity party. All of our helpful happy hormones like dopamine, serotonin, and endorphins are released. Scientists have also found that smiling is contagious (Hatfield et al., 1992). So, you are also making someone else's day better.

2. Take photos of positive things

An excellent practice is to take one photo a day of something positive. Try to make sure that it is not first thing in the morning, tell yourself that there will be something else more positive to snap later. Something very simple like searching for the most positive thing keeps your mind actively looking for the good in the world.

3. Be nice to someone

Our brains have a handy reward system that treats us to a hit of dopamine. When we are kind to others, our brain rewards us. There is a massive feel-good factor for doing something unexpectedly kind for someone else. Bring your colleague a coffee, a massage for your partner, bake a cake for your parents. Try to include at least one act of kindness every day.

4. Start your conversations with positivity

How many times have you started a conversation with a negative comment about the weather? Begin conversations with a positive statement like "I just heard the most amazing song" instead of "I'm never going to get this work done." The conversation will remain lighter and others will perceive you are more positive.

5. Uncancel your plans

It has been heartbreaking to have so many plans canceled due to the pandemic. From holidays to weddings, most of us have felt like life has been put on hold. It might still be a while before we can go through with our plans but that doesn't mean we can't enjoy a taster.

If you had plans to visit Spain, put on some Flamenco music, make a Spanish omelet, and have a Spanish-themed night. Keep learning the language so that you are ready for when the day finally comes.

6. Get specific about your goals

Goals are our motivation. Without them, we plod through life with little drive and little to look forward to. Now that you understand that your brain can continue to learn new things and that anything is possible, it's time to reassess your goals with a more can-do attitude.

Think about the things you have always wanted to do and thought were impossible. Be as specific as possible and include dates for when you want to achieve it. Now create a realistic plan for how you can achieve each goal.

Your goals and plans to achieve them should be written down. The list should contain short-term and long-term goals as well as rewards for each. The rewards are essential because they keep us focused and motivate us when times are hard.

Don't forget to keep reassessing your goals so that you know you are on track.

Don't force positivity. But you should force yourself to make an effort to see the good in your life. And if you really can't find anything, it's essential to start planning something good.

Affirmations vs. Positive Self-Talk

Both affirmations and positive self-talk are methods that encourage the mind to become more optimistic, boost self-esteem and confidence, and be even more productive. These methods are a little delusional for some, but science tells us otherwise.

MRI scans show that when a person repeats a positive affirmation, the brain's reward center is activated. Neurons begin to fire and wire to create pathways in the brain making you happier (Social Cognitive and Affective Neuroscience, 2015).

A study of students showed that learning how to turn their negative self-talk into positive self-talk was a life-impacting skill. Students were able to change their perspectives of themselves and others (Chopra, 2012).

Despite the brain being incredibly clever, it isn't able to distinguish between what is real and what is made up. We know this from experience when we watch a horror movie. The body reacts by increasing the heart rate and tensing muscles even though we are not experiencing what is going on in the scene.

The difference between positive affirmations and positive self-talk is a subtle one. Positive affirmations are short phrases that we repeat, either verbally or in writing. Positive self-talk is a dialogue we have with our subconscious. In both cases, the brain interprets what we say as being real.

A real-life example of how to use affirmations and self-talk would be to start your day with a positive affirmation.

For example, "I have the power to be positive." Throughout the day, you would have conversations with yourself that remind you to look for optimism and, more importantly, to remain positive when things don't go as planned.

I am going to include some examples of affirmations that can also be used as positive self-talk. It's very important that your affirmations and self-talk have meaning to you.

If you read through the list and nothing jumps out at you, you can adapt it so that it is more appealing to you personally or write your own.

If you are creating your own, remember to use the present tense. Just as the brain doesn't decipher between real and made up, it also doesn't react to future tenses. A message about something you will do doesn't cause the brain to react in the moment.

Examples of positive affirmations

- I am worthy of what I desire.

- Good things are coming.

- I am an indestructible powerhouse.

- I am full of energy and joy.

- I rise above.

- I have the energy for all my goals.

- I trust my instincts.

- I see the positives in my life.

Examples of positive self-talk

- This is a thought; this is not my reality. Right now, everything is OK.

- My fear doesn't control me and it doesn't hold me back.

- I haven't reached my goal yet, but I am proud of how far I have come.

- I can learn from this mistake so it doesn't happen again.

- I am in control of my own thoughts, feelings, and actions. These are my responsibilities.

- Each day I am a better version of myself.

- I have the strength and ability to get through this challenge.

- I am a good, kind, smart person who deserves to be happy.

Be sure to make affirmations a part of your routine. You should aim to repeat the affirmation for 3 to 5 minutes, and if possible, 2 or 3 times a day. There is no limit to your positive self-talk. You might need some inspiration before a certain event or task, or it could just be when you are sitting quietly contemplating the world.

If you struggle with positive self-talk, create a persona for your subconscious. Your persona will be determined to fill your mind with negative self-talk. At this point, the negative self-talk won't have the same effects as before and you can put this persona to rest with your positive self-talk.

Why Self-Love, Self-Care, and Self-Appreciation Are Essential

It sounds like a lot of "selfs" and this must be selfish, right? Absolutely not! A selfish person is constantly putting their own needs and pleasures in front of others and having no regard for others. Here are what these 3 self-concepts are about:

- **Self-love:** The ability to recognize and appreciate your emotions. It also means putting your physical and mental needs before those of others.

- **Self-care:** Becoming the best version of yourself; looking after yourself so that you are able to look after others.

- **Self-appreciation:** Appreciating that we all have good in us; taking the time to see who we are in this moment.

From here on in, we will combine the 3 into self-care. The reason why self-care is so important and not selfish is that we all have some form of responsibility.

We have bills to pay, children or parents to take care of, a job, friends who need us. If we don't take care of ourselves, it is impossible to take care of our responsibilities.

When these responsibilities get left behind, we subject ourselves to more stress, pressure, negativity, anxiety, and depression.

Between December 2015 and March 2016, 871 medical students completed self-reports on both their self-care and quality of life. Researchers looked at both physical and psychological stress.

The more self-care the students practiced, the greater the decrease in perceived stress and they were more resilient (Ayala et al., 2018).

The pandemic has also significantly increased the need for self-care as many of our responsibilities have taken a rapid change. Teaching your children from home is a whole different responsibility. Running extra errands for loved ones so they can self-isolate adds strain to your life.

Ideas for self-care are endless and may be personal. Not everyone is going to find 20 minutes in the bathtub as a chance to recharge their batteries. Others would hate the idea of getting a massage or running 5 miles.

Nevertheless, your health depends on implementing as many of the following tips as possible.

1. Eat a well-balanced diet

You don't need to be on a permanent diet. However, fruits and vegetables will provide the nutrients your body needs, carbohydrates give you the energy, and omega-3s (found in fatty fish, nuts, and seeds) are excellent brain food.

Try not to just treat food as a source of fuel. Because of our busy lifestyles, cooking is often seen as an additional burden rather than a task to enjoy. It will be good for your diet and your brain to learn a new recipe each week and have fun at the same time.

2. Exercise

Exercise helps control your weight, improves heart health, and reduces the chances of numerous illnesses and diseases. It reduces stress, boosts happy hormones, and helps with sleep quality.

Both the Mayo Clinic and NHS recommend 150 minutes of moderate aerobic exercise or 75 minutes of vigorous aerobic exercise a week.

Start off small, even if it's just a 10-minute walk each day. You can build on this and gradually make the activity more intense.

3. Get the right amount of sleep

Some people need 8 hours, others do just as well on 6 hours. Create a strong bedtime routine that starts at least half an hour before you need to sleep. As we have said, it might be obvious to say avoid coffee but if you have issues sleeping, you might want to avoid any caffeine after 3 p.m.

Also, as tempted as you are, leave mobile devices out of the bedroom. Screens produce a blue light which prevents melatonin from being produced. Melatonin is the hormone we need to fall asleep.

4. Drink plenty of water

I know that this isn't anything new but understanding the science behind it will motivate you to drink more.

Depending on age and gender, the body is 50 to 75% water. The brain is 85% water. Drinking 7 ounces of water (about 200 ml) an hour can halve the number of mistakes we make.

When hydration falls to less than 2% of body weight, your mood can be affected (Water Plus, n.d.).

5. Take regular breaks

You might think that cramming in hours of work is productive. Most people are only capable of concentrating for up to 90 minutes at a time. After this, it is better to walk away from the desk and the screen for a few minutes.

You may also want to consider changing up your work environment. If you have an area to use a standing desk or if you have phone calls to make, walk around for a while. A sedentary 8 hours of work is draining and terrible for your body.

Drink a glass of water when you wake up and before you go to bed. Set an alarm as a reminder to drink water throughout the day. You can add slices of fruit to a water bottle to add flavor if you get bored of just water.

6. Learn how to say no

If we can't say no, all of our time is going to be filled with things that other people require and self-care gets put off or ignored. Sometimes we have to accept the fact that we can't do everything and stay well. Saying no is not unkind, it's a method of self-protection.

Being assertive will help you say no in a way that doesn't offend the other person and doesn't allow them to try and change your mind. Keep your no short and don't feel the need to justify why you can't do what the other person wants. You can offer a solution or alternative if your schedule allows.

7. Make time for the things you love

Before we became far too serious about life, there were a great number of activities that we loved and made us laugh and feel good. Think back to what you used to do as a child, maybe it was football or basketball practice, rollerblading, or hanging out with your pets.

Look for groups or clubs in your area that offer activities you might want to try. You don't have to make a life-long commitment. But it's great to explore new hobbies and find out what makes you happy now.

8. Get organized

Just one thing like losing your keys in the morning can affect your stress levels for the rest of the day. Forgetting passwords costs you time. Missing meetings and plans is irresponsible.

Getting more organized is a small change that adds structure to your routine and helps you remain in control. Use apps, calendars, and lists to keep yourself organized. Keep the important items that you need every day (like keys, chargers, purses, etc.) in the same place.

It sounds like self-care takes a lot of time and time is already short. You need to schedule in self-care time, even if it's just 30 minutes twice a week or 10 minutes every morning. Make it a solid rule that this time is for you and you only.

What will happen is that you will soon start feeling better and more energized. Things like doing the weekly grocery shop aren't as draining and it gets easier to wake up a little earlier to squeeze in more exercise. You will get more done during the working hours, so you aren't having to work later in the evenings. Self-care is crucial for work-life balance!

Automate Your Positive Thoughts

Remember negativity bias? The ability to remember the bad over the good because each time we relive a bad moment, the neurons in the brain are fired up, get wired together, and become stronger?

If we can use science to break the negativity bias and stop thinking about the negative, we can use the same science to automate positive thinking.

Think of this, you have just had a great night out with friends. You danced, laughed, and this is the best you have felt in a long time. You go home and think about the night. In the morning, you remember a song that you danced to and it makes you smile. During the day, you think about your friend's terrible moves...and you laugh again.

Every time you think about your amazing night out, neurons in the brain are firing and making new memories. If you do the same for all the good things in your life, your memories become more positive.

This isn't just going to help your brain to automatically think more positively. It's going to help with your decision-making and problem-solving skills. We access the memories of our past experiences to resolve current issues. If a friend invited you out and your past experience was a bad one, your decision will be based on this negativity and it's more likely that you say no—limiting your new experiences.

If your brain has the ability to automatically think negatively, it has the ability to automatically think positively. You have to teach it how!

Why and How to Live in the Moment

If you have done any research into negative thinking, you will have seen that almost everybody recommends meditation and for a very good reason. Meditation and mindfulness will help with every issue we have discussed from depression to sleep, intrusive thoughts to stress management.

Like affirmations and positive thinking, meditation may sound like the latest solution to fix all of our problems. But if something has been used for thousands of years, it's hard to deny its effectiveness.

Meditation has been used for centuries as a way of living in the present. By taking time each day to enjoy the here and now, we are not distracted by the worries of our past and future.

Being mindful of the present enables us to stay grounded, reduce stress levels, and helps us cope with our negative thoughts and emotions. It gives us a moment to appreciate the little things in life that can make us happy and the amazing things that are in the world if we look hard enough.

There are plenty of studies to choose from to see the positive impact of mindful meditation to be more in the present. According to Mindful (2018), meditation has been proven to sharpen our focus, improve mental health, strengthen our relationships, and even reduce bias.

The present deserves more credit! It's the only moment we have that has no time. It's what separates our past and future. You will never get this present moment back again. So, how do we start to enjoy the present? Mindful meditation.

1. Dedicate the right amount of time. In the beginning, this will only be a few minutes as you are learning. Make sure you won't be interrupted and turn your phone off.

2. Meditation doesn't have to be sitting down with crossed legs. You can sit, lay, even walk, as long as you are comfortable.

3. Pay attention to your body. Are your muscles relaxed? Do you need to move position so that the tension will be released?

4. Turn your senses to the present. Mindful meditation isn't about silencing the mind, it's about letting the mind pay attention to what is happening. Focus on the light and the heat on your skin. What can you hear and smell?

5. Take a slow deep breath in, allow it to fill all of your belly before you exhale. Keep concentrating on your breathing. Count the breaths if it helps.

6. The mind will start to wander. Don't judge yourself for this, it's normal. Allow the thought to come and go but don't pay it any unnecessary attention. Visualize it as the thought floats away again.

7. Bring your attention back to your breathing. Each time your mind wanders, accept the thought and return to your breathing.

The goal will be to gradually increase the time you meditate for up to 10 to 20 minutes per day. You can start off by doing a few minutes, 2 or 3 times a day or when you need it. Any time I speak in front of a large group, I will take a few minutes just to be mindful. Don't just give up after a day or two. It can take a few weeks to start noticing the benefits of mindful meditation.

It sounds like a simple practice. But quieting the brain so that you can accept thoughts but not let them take control is a lot harder to master than it sounds. There are also so many different types of meditation that you might need a little help looking for the one that suits you best.

Look at some of the best meditation apps to get you started. Headspace, Aura, and Smiling Mind are three excellent examples. There are also thousands of guided meditation videos online, the voice will help you focus.

A Simple Way to Turn Your Toxic Thoughts into Positive Actions

The toxic thoughts are the nastiest kind of thoughts, whether about yourself or someone else. They provide us with no value, which means the only thing they are going to achieve is self-doubt, negative self-talk, rumination, and negative spiraling.

As your confidence and self-esteem grow, you will have fewer toxic thoughts about yourself. In the meantime, we are going to use these toxic thoughts to motivate us to make the changes we need to see. We can do this by incorporating our toxic thoughts into our positive self-talk. Here are some examples:

• I'm ugly: I'm ugly when I frown so I need to remember to smile more.

• I'm never going to lose this weight: I'm going to increase my aerobic activity by X to lose Y by Z.

• I won't get the promotion because I'm not smart enough: If I take this online course, I can have the same qualifications as my colleagues. If I take two online classes, I will be more qualified.

- I hate the way my friend is always making fun of me: My new thicker skin will prevent my friend's words from hurting me while I learn to be more assertive.

Most people think that anger is a bad emotion. Anger is neither good nor bad, it's what we do with it that makes all the difference. Toxic thoughts can stir up many emotions, pity, shame, guilt, frustration, and disappointment are just a few. What if we could turn a toxic thought into anger and use this anger for good.

Don't let your toxic thoughts cause you to dwell. Get angry about them. Your parents don't have the right to micromanage your life. Your boss can't manipulate you into working overtime. You are not a bad person. Get angry about these things and use this anger to create energy that will push you into action.

When we are angry about something, it is because we care. Global issues like climate change, racism, and gender violence can spark very toxic thoughts. But, instead of assuming that this is the world we live in, wouldn't it be better to get angry and do something about it?

If someone is mistreating you, don't play the victim, don't accept it. Get angry, go for a workout to clear your head, boost all of the necessary hormones and go and tell this person that you won't take it anymore.

Remember that you control your anger, the anger doesn't control you. This technique is left for later on in the book because it would be considered a more advanced technique. You need to be fully aware of your emotions and know how to calm down after getting angry.

If you can't control your emotions, you risk acting on the anger. Only use anger as the kick in the bum to get you into positive action.

Put It into Practice

For this practice, we need 15 minutes. I know this sounds like a lot but there are still 1,425 minutes in the day to get everything else done. These 15 minutes are going to be the crucial 15 minutes that start your day on the right foot and all you need to do is get up 15 minutes earlier.

Begin by taking a couple of deep breaths. Stretch your muscles, paying close attention to your neck, shoulders, and spine. Now choose a vigorous aerobic exercise such as skipping, jumping jacks, or running on the spot. Choose another low aerobic activity like walking on the spot or dancing.

We are going to do 30 seconds of high impact followed by 1 minute of low impact. Repeat this 4 times. Follow this up with some more stretches. Next, get comfortable and finish off with a few minutes of mindful meditation. Finish off your 15 minutes with a positive affirmation or a gratitude statement.

After a shower and fresh clothes, you will be in the perfect place physically and mentally for the day. If you are already an active person, you might find that you can do more, which is great. The idea right now is to make a start, without the need for any equipment or excuses. Once you make a start and it becomes a part of your routine, you can start making small changes to extend the intensity and time.

CONCLUSION

Y ou have every right to feel the way you do. Life is hard and we are faced with a mountain of challenges that we think we don't have the strength or ability to get through. You aren't alone. But like so many other people, you have the choice to make a change and leave the negativity behind you.

You also don't need to feel overwhelmed by all of the information, techniques, and ideas that are in this book. There are more techniques than you will need for a good reason.

We are all individuals, and some strategies will work better for some than others. You will probably have read some ideas that really stick out in your mind.

Try to take a couple from each section to get you started. Start small. Just because there are more than 30 ideas, doesn't mean you need to implement them all.

If you have tried all of the techniques, or there is absolutely no way to start seeing any progress, please visit your doctor. It may be that your problems have become so deep-rooted that you need some additional help. All of the techniques in this book can be used alongside the solutions your doctor provides.

Let's recap L.I.B.E.R.T.Y. and some of the key takeaways of each.

The first step on this journey was to **Learn** how the brain works. Negativity bias is unfortunate because it makes it more difficult to fight the flood of negative thoughts. However, we have also learned that this way of thinking can be broken. This first chapter required self-reflection and an understanding of where our negative thinking and rumination stem from.

Inspect our thought patterns opened our eyes to the various mental models that can be used to expand the way we think. We saw simple tools that we could use to understand how we view the world and our life. The intuitive tool that requires you to list your own example for each of the 12 types of negative thought is ideal to get a clearer appreciation of how negative thinking is more complex than just being pessimistic.

This led us to the chapter to **Beat** our negative thinking. The 10 categories looked at how you can make just a few changes to your home to create a more positive environment. We examined the growth mindset and how to create it.

For this section, I find it extremely useful to pay a little extra attention to the downward spiraling negative thoughts. They are especially painful because, like the rock rolling down a mountain, they quickly gain momentum and power.

From talking to clients, friends, family, and readers, the majority of people feel that if they could just get a little more sleep, they would have more energy to handle negativity.

This is why the chapter on **Eliminate** rumination is the foundation for wiping the slate clean; remembering that the past and future cannot dictate our present and nor can the opinions of others.

It's the inner critic that has become the ringmaster of our thoughts that we addressed in the chapter to **Rewire** the brain.

My personal favorite will always be a complete declutter to help calm the business in the brain. Still, the instant tips that have been proven by neuroscientists (splashing your face with cold water) have helped me time and time again.

Throw away negativity and **Yield** positive results are saved for the end for good reasons. First, you don't eat your dessert before your mains, and second, you need to work on the first 5 steps so that you are in a better, stronger position to embrace the positive.

The last thing you can probably imagine right now is finding the energy to exercise when you can barely drag yourself out of bed. This might be one of the biggest battles you have with your mentality. But you have to win this battle. Remember that it's not about just getting up and going out for a run or joining the gym.

We always have to start small in every change we make. Starting small might just be a short walk, jogging on the spot in your home, or 5 minutes of yoga with the help of an app.

The hardest part isn't the first day. The hardest part will be the daily battle until it becomes a routine. But, becoming more physically active will change the way you see yourself and the events in your life.

Like exercise, meditation will provide more benefits to your physical and mental health than you could have originally thought. Again, it takes time, and you need to feel positive about meditation before you begin. If you tell your mind it won't work, your mind will believe you.

And the mind is the most amazing tool you have. It is flexible, it believes what you tell it, whether that's physical or mental messages. Science has shown us that we are all capable of change, as long as we want it. If you have got to the end of this book, it's very clear that you want this change.

Use this desire and determination to follow through with the small changes you make. Don't let that negative persona tell you that what you are doing isn't working.

The techniques work when you give them time. Be firm with your negative persona but kind to yourself. Take time to enjoy the things that you do. Even the most mundane tasks like cleaning can be turned into a positive with the right mindset.

I have the utmost confidence in you, and I know that you can start leading a more positive life with the help of this book. You have done so well even making the choice to stop your negative thinking. I genuinely love to hear how people are turning their lives around and I would be extremely grateful if you could leave a short review on Amazon so that others who are struggling can learn that there is light at the end of the tunnel.

SOME BOOKS YOU MAY FIND INTERESTING

How to Stop Overthinking

The 7-Step Plan to Control and Eliminate Negative Thoughts, Declutter Your Mind and Start Thinking Positively in 5 Minutes or Less

Do you find yourself lying awake at night because you can't stop worrying about what happened today? Are you constantly second-guessing almost every decision that you are faced with in life?

By reading this book, you will emboldened yourself to deal with your fears, anxiety, and stop your overthinking for good.

What you should expect along the journey of practicing the techniques and strategies throughout this book is to be aware of where your mental chatter comes from, and how to address it.

Stop worrying about what you did today and start living in the moment. Stop living for tomorrow and start breathing in the positivity of today.

Stop overthinking your future and make big changes to live your future now.

What you'll learn:

• How to Control Overthinking and Eliminate Negative Thoughts in Just a Few Minutes.

• 10 Powerful Tactics to Stop Anxiety and Worrying Permanently.

• How to Sleep Better, Even if Your Head Is Full of Thoughts.

• Simple Tips to Develop Self-Confidence and Decision-Making Skills.

• How to Remove Toxicity and Change Your Relationships for the Better.

• 5 Ways to Calm Anxiety (Worrying) in Five Minutes or Less.

• Troubleshooting Guide if Nothing Helps.

• How to Declutter Your Mind and Become What You Want in Life.

So, quit being stuck, stop letting your mind trap you, and take control of what you want.

Would You Like To Know More?

Grab this book to get started and turn off your overthinking for good!

Scan the QR code below to order it from Amazon immediately.

Healthy Boundaries

How to Set Strong Boundaries, Say No Without Guilt, and Maintain Good Relationships With Your Parents, Family, and Friends

Discover the power of self-love, and learn how to set healthy boundaries -- without feeling guilty.

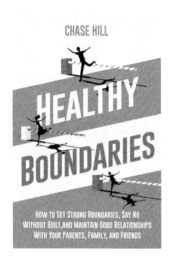

Do you ever wonder what it would be like if the people you care about respected your personal space? Do you wish that there was an easy way to say "No" every time you don't want to say "Yes"?

If this is you, then you've probably had moments of trying to please others -- often, to your own detriment.

Perhaps you have an inability to say "No" because you don't want to disappoint or anger the other person... leading you to do things you never wanted to do in the first place...

If this happens too often, eventually, people will start taking you for granted – and you won't be taken seriously even when you try to say "No."

What's worse, when you do try to set up boundaries, people will label you as mean or moody.

But there's a simple way to solve your problems!

You can start doing what YOU want to do. You don't have to compromise your individuality just to be "considerate" of others.

You can set healthy boundaries, and make your friends, family and parents **respect that boundary.**

In *Healthy Boundaries*, here's just a taste of what you'll discover:

• **A step-by-step guide to setting healthy personal boundaries without starting an argument**

• The secret to saying "No" **without feeling guilty** -- and without being misunderstood

• How to stop constantly apologizing, and find out when you should and shouldn't be sorry

• 10 debilitating myths that are stopping you from setting up boundaries -- and how to troubleshoot them

• How to detoxify your emotions and release toxicity from your system like a breath of fresh air

• **A clear path** to give you the freedom to love yourself, follow what YOU want, and prioritize yourself

If you're ready to start living the life you deserve without feeling guilty, then scan this QR code right now!

Assertiveness Training

How to Stand Up for Yourself, Boost Your Confidence, and Improve Assertive Communication Skills

Stop being a pushover — it's time for you to be seen, be heard, and to get what you deserve.

Have you spent the better portion of your life physically and mentally unable to strive for what you **really want**, passively riding the waves as they come?

Are you constantly considerate of others' feelings, having made too many compromises in the past that have left you feeling unfulfilled and empty?

You may currently be facing an unsettling internal conflict, wondering how you can assert yourself and express your **genuine** thoughts, needs, and opinions without being aggressive or disliked by those around you.

Being assertive isn't synonymous with being aggressive or unfriendly — it is very much possible to be confident and firm all while being **polite and kind**.

There's no reason to be held back by discomfort and fear anymore — with the right training, your timid nature will undoubtedly subside, making room for the assertive person you've always longed to be.

In *Assertiveness Training*, you will discover:

• How to recognize the **subtle behaviors** that have been hindering your path to self-fulfillment

• **Scientifically proven** steps to practice self-awareness and emotional control to avoid the most common emotional setbacks barricading the way between you and your assertive self

• How to tackle the anxiety and fear that come from your first attempts at being assertive, **making assertiveness second nature**

• A plethora of situation-based tips and tricks that will guide you through the process of knowing exactly what to say and do to let people know that you're not to be walked over

• **Comprehensive guidance** on how to be assertive in your workplace to finally get the recognition and respect you deserve

• A step-by-step **action plan**, taking you on a transformative journey towards building more confidence

Assertiveness is not a natural-born trait, but it is a skill that we all can acquire with perseverance and the right kind of guidance.

It's time to gain the respect and admiration of others for being who you truly are.

How to Read People Like a Book

Speed-Read, Analyze, and Understand Anyone's Body Language, Emotions, and Thoughts

Stop racking your brain to figure out what others are really trying to say... know how to instantly decode the meaning behind their unspoken messages.

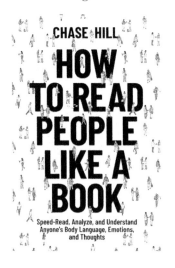

You don't have to be a communication expert, detective, or superhero to learn how to recognize and decode social cues. All you need to do is to know exactly what to look for and what they really mean.

Fortunately, this book contains everything you need to know about deciphering other people's silent messages.

Inside, here is just a fraction of what you will discover:

- How to interpret facial expressions, body language, tone of voice, and other nonverbal cues – spare yourself from any miscommunication!

- **50+ social cues that will clue you in on what a person is thinking or feeling**... no more guessing games that could lead you to trouble

- What "clusters of gestures" are and why they are crucial to reading other people

- **25+ effective ways to tell if someone's lying — make any seasoned detective proud with your skills**

- Factors that affect how you read people — avoid getting the wrong conclusion about someone!

- **How to read between the lines using verbal cues… their choice of words matters more than you think!**

- Fool-proof ways to identify the tone of a text or email

And much more.

Every day, you encounter dozens of social cues without knowing how powerful they are or how you can use them to your advantage.

It's time to flip the narrative — by learning how to accurately read other people, you will not just boost your communication skills… you'll foster deeper connections and enjoy improved relationships more than ever.

Master the art of nonverbal communication and read people like a pro.

YOUR FREE EBOOK

29 WAYS TO OVERCOME NEGATIVE THOUGHTS

I'd like to give you a gift as a way of saying thanks for your purchase!

In 29 Ways to Overcome Negative Thoughts, you'll discover:

- 10 Strategies to Reduce Negativity in Your Life
- 7 Steps to Quickly Stop Negative Thoughts
- 12 Powerful Tips to Beat Negative Thinking

To receive your Free Ebook, visit the link:

free.chasehillbooks.com

Alternatively, you can scan the QR-code below:

If you have any difficulty downloading the ebook, contact me at **chase@chasehillbooks.com,** and I'll send you a copy as soon as possible.

REFERENCES

Anxiety & Depression Association of America. (n.d.-a). *Facts & Statistics | Anxiety and Depression Association of America, ADAA*. ADAA. Retrieved October 12, 2021, from https://adaa.org/understanding-anxiety/facts-statistics

Anxiety & Depression Association of America. (n.d.-b). *Social Anxiety Disorder | Anxiety and Depression Association of America, ADAA*. ADAA. Retrieved October 12, 2021, from https://adaa.org/understanding-anxiety/social-anxiety-disorder

BBC. (2021, March 5). *Neuroplasticity: How to rewire your brain*. BBC Reel. https://www.bbc.com/reel/video/p098v92g/neuroplasticity-how-to-rewire-your-brain

Bothered by Negative, Unwanted Thoughts? Just Throw Them Away. (2012, November 26). Association for Psychological Science - APS. https://www.psychologicalscience.org/news/releases/bothered-by-negative-unwanted-thoughts-just-throw-them-away.html

Bradt, S. (2010, November 11). *Wandering mind not a happy mind*. Harvard Gazette. https://news.harvard.edu/gazette/story/2010/11/wandering-mind-not-a-happy-mind/

Bright, R. M. (2012, October 29). *Impact of positive self-talk.* OPUS. https://opus.uleth.ca/handle/10133/3202

Brooker, H. (2019, July 1). *The relationship between the frequency of numberâpuzzle use and baseline cognitive function in a large online sample of adults aged 50 and over.* Wiley Online Library. https://onlinelibrary.wiley.com/doi/abs/10.1002/gps.5085

Cacioppo, J. T. (2014, June 27). *The negativity bias: Conceptualization, quantification, and individual differences | Behavioral and Brain Sciences.* Cambridge Core. https://www.cambridge.org/core/journals/behavioral-and-brain-sciences/article/abs/negativity-bias-conceptualization-quantification-and-individual-differences/3EB6EF536DB5B7CF34508F8979F3210E

Camacho, L. (2019, February 26). *Four Ways Negativity Bias Slows You Down (And How To Stop It).* Forbes. https://www.forbes.com/sites/forbescoachescouncil/2019/02/26/four-ways-negativity-bias-slows-you-down-and-how-to-stop-it/?sh=27fb3cf2c5f9

Cascio, C. N. (2015, November 5). *Self-affirmation activates brain systems associated with self-related processing and reward and is reinforced by future orientation.* NCBI NLM NIH. https://www.ncbi.nlm.nih.gov/pmc/articles/PMC4814782/

Castillo, B. B., & Nolan, C. (2019, April 3). *Deepak Chopra: How to rewire your brain for success.* CNBC. https://www.cnbc.com/video/2019/04/03/deepak-chopra-how-to-rewire-your-brain-for-success.html

Chapman Ph.D., B. P. (2013, July 14). *Emotion Suppression and Mortality Risk Over a 12-Year Follow-up*. NCBI NLM NIH. https://www.ncbi.nlm.nih.gov/pmc/articles/PMC3939772/

Cirino, E. (2019, April 18). *10 Tips to Help You Stop Ruminating*. Healthline. https://www.healthline.com/health/how-to-stop-ruminating#tips

Cohen, L. G. (1998, July). *Studies of neuroplasticity with transcranial magnetic stimulation*. PubMed. https://pubmed.ncbi.nlm.nih.gov/9736465/

Farnam Street. (2021, June 2). *Mental Models: The Best Way to Make Intelligent Decisions (~100 Models Explained)*. https://fs.blog/mental-models/

FBI. (2021, June 14). *Uniform Crime Reporting (UCR) Program*. Federal Bureau of Investigation. https://www.fbi.gov/services/cjis/ucr

Frothingham, S. (2019, October 24). *How Long Does It Take for a New Behavior to Become Automatic?* Healthline. https://www.healthline.com/health/how-long-does-it-take-to-form-a-habit

Goldstein, M. (2021, March 2). *How to Control Your Thoughts and Be the Master of Your Mind*. Lifehack. https://www.lifehack.org/articles/lifestyle/how-to-master-your-mind-part-one-whos-running-your-thoughts.html

Harvard University. (n.d.). *Identifying Negative Automatic Thought Patterns*. Stress & Development Lab. Retrieved October 12, 2021, from https://sdlab.fas.harvard.edu/cognitive-reappraisal/identifying-negative-automatic-thought-patterns

Heckman, W. (2019, September 25). *42 Worrying Workplace Stress Statistics*. The American Institute of Stress. https://www.stress.org/42-worrying-workplace-stress-statistics

Jeffrey, S. (2020, June 23). *Change Your Fixed Mindset into a Growth Mindset [Complete Guide]*. Scott Jeffrey. https://scottjeffrey.com/change-your-fixed-mindset/#A_4-Step_Process_to_Change_Your_Mindset

Kim, E. S. (2017, January 4). *Optimism and Cause -Specific Mortality: A Prospective Cohort Study*. Oxford Academic. https://academic.oup.com/aje/article/185/1/21/2631298

Koeck, M.D., P. (n.d.). *How does our brain process negative thoughts?* 15Minutes4Me. Retrieved October 12, 2021, from https://www.15minutes4me.com/depression/how-does-our-brain-process-negative-thoughts

Kurland Ph.D., B. (2018, September 13). *Reversing the Downward Spiral*. Psychology Today. https://www.psychologytoday.com/us/blog/the-well-being-toolkit/201809/reversing-the-downward-spiral

LaFreniere, A. S., & Newman, M. G. (2020, May 1). *Exposing Worryâs Deceit: Percentage of Untrue Worries in Generalized Anxiety Disorder Treatment*. ScienceDirect. https://www.sciencedirect.com/science/article/abs/pii/S0005789419300826

M. (2021, April 5). *8 Ways to Stop Taking Things Personally*. Dare to Live Fully. https://daringtolivefully.com/stop-taking-things-personally

Mackenzie, C.H.T., Ph.D., L. (n.d.). *Take A Hidden Negativity Test by Linda Mackenzie*. Linda Mackenzie's Mind Center. Retrieved October 12, 2021, from http://www.lindamackenzie.net/hiddennegativitytest.htm

Maloney, B. (2020, January 22). *The Damaging Effects of Negativity by Bree Maloney*. Marque Medical. https://marquemedical.com/damaging-effects-of-negativity/

Manchester City Council. (2019, August 29). *'Ey up petal – how docs are prescribing plants to keep Mancs (k)ale and hearty*. Healthier Manchester. https://healthiermanchester.org/ey-up-petal-how-docs-are-prescribing-plants-to-keep-mancs-kale-and-hearty/

National Institute of Mental Health. (n.d.). *NIMH » Social Anxiety Disorder: More Than Just Shyness*. NIMH. Retrieved October 12, 2021, from https://www.nimh.nih.gov/health/publications/social-anxiety-disorder-more-than-just-shyness

NeuroImage. (2015, January 15). *The artist emerges: Visual art learning alters neural structure and function*. ScienceDirect. https://www.sciencedirect.com/science/article/abs/pii/S1053811914009318

New Neuroscience Reveals 4 Easy Rituals That Will Make You Stress-Free. (2017, June 11). Barking Up The Wrong Tree. https://www.bakadesuyo.com/2017/02/stress-free/

NHS website. (2021, August 4). *5 steps to mental wellbeing*. Nhs.Uk. https://www.nhs.uk/mental-health/self-help/guides-tools-and-activities/five-steps-to-mental-wellbeing/

Nittle, N. (2021, July 2). *Can Social Media Cause Depression?* Verywell Mind. https://www.verywellmind.com/social-media-and-depression-5085354

Raypole, C. (2020, March 17). *Meet Anticipatory Anxiety, The Reason You Worry About Things That Haven't Happened Yet.* Healthline. https://www.healthline.com/health/anticipatory-anxiety#coping-tips

Riggio Ph.D., R. E. (2012, June 25). *There's Magic in Your Smile.* Psychology Today. https://www.psychologytoday.com/us/blog/cutting-edge-leadership/201206/there-s-magic-in-your-smile

Robson, D. (2020, August 18). *The 'Batman Effect': How having an alter ego empowers you.* BBC Worklife. https://www.bbc.com/worklife/article/20200817-the-batman-effect-how-having-an-alter-ego-empowers-you

Ryan, T. (2021, May 20). *The Best Essential Oils for Sleep.* Sleep Foundation. https://www.sleepfoundation.org/best-essential-oils-for-sleep

Sabxe, D. E., & Repetti, R. (2009, November 23). *SAGE Journals: Your gateway to world-class research journals.* SAGE Journals. https://journals.sagepub.com/action/cookieAbsent

Sánchez-Vidaña, D. I. (2017). *The Effectiveness of Aromatherapy for Depressive Symptoms: A Systematic Review.* PubMed Central (PMC). https://www.ncbi.nlm.nih.gov/pmc/articles/PMC5241490/

Sanju, H. K. (2015, December). *Neuroplasticity In Musicians Brain:Review.* Research Gate. https://www.research-gate.net/publication/286451613_Neuroplasticity_In_Musicians_BrainReview

Santos-Longhurst, A. (2018, August 31). *High Cortisol Symptoms: What Do They Mean?* Healthline. https://www.healthline.com/health/high-cortisol-symptoms#meaning

Scale of the Human Brain. (2020, December 11). AI Impacts. https://aiimpacts.org/scale-of-the-human-brain/

Scheier, M. F., & Carver, C. S. (2019, December 1). *Dispositional Optimism and Physical Health: A Long Look Back, A Quick Look Forward.* NCBI NLM NIH. https://www.ncbi.nlm.nih.gov/pmc/articles/PMC6309621/

Scully, S. M. (2020, July 22). *'Toxic Positivity' Is Real — and It's a Big Problem During the Pandemic.* Healthline. https://www.healthline.com/health/mental-health/toxic-positivity-during-the-pandemic#So,-how-do-you-deal-with-toxic-positivity

Sethi, S. (2020, October 7). *How to Tone Your Vagus Nerve and Why You Should.* Dr. Shelly Sethi. https://www.drshelly-sethi.com/2020/02/how-to-tone-your-vagus-nerve-and-why-you-should/

Skoyles, C. (2021, January 12). *5 Breathing Exercises for Anxiety (Simple and Calm Anxiety Quickly).* Lifehack. https://www.life-hack.org/761526/breathing-exercises-for-anxiety-simple-and-calm-anxiety-quickly

Staff, N. (2020, October 12). *Tips to Help Stop Intrusive Thoughts*. Northpoint Recovery's Blog. https://www.northpointrecovery.com/blog/7-tips-deal-stop-intrusive-thoughts/

Stillman, J. (2021, January 5). *Bill Gates Always Reads Before Bed. Science Suggests You Should Too*. Inc.Com. https://www.inc.com/jessica-stillman/bill-gates-always-reads-for-an-hour-before-bed-science-suggests-you-should-do-same.html

the Healthline Editorial Team. (2020, April 7). *The Benefits of Vitamin D*. Healthline. https://www.healthline.com/health/food-nutrition/benefits-vitamin-d#fights-disease

Wegner, D. M. (1987, July). *Paradoxical effects of thought suppression*. PubMed. https://pubmed.ncbi.nlm.nih.gov/3612492/

What to Know About 4-7-8 Breathing. (2021, June 14). WebMD. https://www.webmd.com/balance/what-to-know-4-7-8-breathing

Why we should drink water at work. (n.d.). Water Plus Limited. Retrieved October 12, 2021, from https://www.waterplus.co.uk/fresh-thinking-hub/why-we-should-drink-water-at-work

Wolff, C. (2019, March 18). *How Negativity Actually Messes With Your Brain Chemistry*. FabFitFun. https://fabfitfun.com/magazine/negativity-effects-brain-chemistry/

Wong, Y. J. (2016, May 3). *Does gratitude writing improve the mental health of psychotherapy clients? Evidence from a randomized controlled trial.* Taylor & Francis. https://www.tandfonline.-com/doi/abs/10.1080/10503307.2016.1169332?scroll=top&needAccess=true&journalCode=tpsr20